W9-BUF-093

PERRY ISLAND

Perry River

Chantrey Inlet

Cockburn Bay

Franklin Lake

Back River

Repulse Bay

VICTORIA ISLAND

Garry Lake

Wager Bay

Pelly Lake

Back River

(D I S T R I C T   o f   K E E W A T I N)

Lunan Lake

Beverly Lake

Aberdeen Lake

Schultz Lake

Thelon River

Sugarloaf Mt. +

BAKER LAKE

Baker Lake

Chesterfield Inlet

HUDSON BAY

Kazan River

CHESTERFIELD INLET

GJOA HAVEN

N U N A V U T

APPROX. NORTHERN TREELINE LIMIT

CHESTERFIELD INLET

HUDSON BAY

SASKATCHEWAN

MANITOBA

CHURCHILL

WALKING ON THE LAND

KEY PORTER BOOKS

Walking on

Farley Mowat

the Land

Canadian Cataloguing in Publication Data

Mowat, Farley, 1921–
    Walking on the land

ISBN 1-55263-167-2

1. Inuit – History – Fiction. I. Title.

PS8526.089W34 2000   C813'.54   C00-931643-4
PR9199.3.M68W34 2000

THE CANADA COUNCIL | LE CONSEIL DES ARTS
FOR THE ARTS | DU CANADA
SINCE 1957 | DEPUIS 1957

The publisher gratefully acknowledges the support of the Canada Council for the Arts and the Ontario Arts Council for its publishing program.

We acknowledge the financial support of the Government of Canada through the Book Publishing Industry Development Program (BPIDP) for our publishing activities.

Key Porter Books Limited
70 The Esplanade
Toronto, Ontario
Canada M5E 1R2

www.keyporter.com

Design: Peter Maher
Electronic formatting: Heidy Lawrance Associates

Printed and bound in Canada

00 01 02 03 04 6 5 4 3 2 1

For Elisapee and her people,
and for Claire, who makes all things possible.

Table of Contents

WALKING ON THE LAND

Prologue

On a summer's day in 1999 our aging Labrador announced the arrival of a visitor to our Cape Breton farmstead.

Nothing unusual in that. My wife, Claire, and I receive many visitors.

However, this was an exceptional one. The small, solidly built, black-haired woman with darting eyes and gleaming smile who stepped tentatively out of a rental car was from another time.

She was Elisapee—a name given to her at three years of age when she was thrust into our world from another, older one. There she had been called Nurrahaq. Her people were Inuit whom I had met in 1947 and again in 1948. The *Ihalmiut*—People from Beyond—were inland dwellers with no knowledge of the sea and little of modern times. Nurrahaq was the youngest daughter of a woman named Kikik, whose tormented latter days impinged on my days for more than a decade.

Although Elisapee grew up on the fringes of the ancient Ihalmiut lands, and in the company of other Inuit, she was nevertheless walled off from her origins because the few remaining adult Ihalmiut believed the phantoms of the past could best be dealt with by consigning memory of them to limbo.

When Elisapee Karetak—her married name—was in her early thirties, she felt compelled to enter that place of shadows but was advised, "Leave it alone. It is all over now. It is nothing to you now."

Elisapee might have obeyed these injunctions. Nurrahaq would not. So Kikik's child embarked on a search "for understanding of what I was ... of who my people were ... of why I had no past."

Severe disapproval from her compatriots and peers frustrated her early efforts. Yet she persisted with such intensity as to alienate her from her own community and threaten her health.

It was at this juncture that a worn copy of a book of mine, *The Desperate People*, published in 1959, made its way to the Arctic village of Arviat (formerly Eskimo Point), where Elisapee was living. In it she found an account of the ordeals endured by her mother and her people, and something of their history.

Heartened by this discovery, she eventually travelled from her home on the western coast of Hudson Bay to mine on the eastern seaboard of North America, determined to add whatever I might know to her knowledge of a forgotten and forbidden past.

Many others assisted Elisapee in her search. Foremost among them was Ole Gjerstad, a documentary film-maker from Montreal who became Elisapee's champion. Such was his capacity for sympathetic mediation that the situation in Arviat underwent a sea change and the barriers between past and present were overthrown. Elisapee and the other surviving Ihalmiut became one again, and together they resurrected memories of other times, not as tales of suffering and guilt but as testimony to the indomitable spirit of their kind.

Elisapee and Gjerstad co-produced a docudrama about her mother's life.[1] Much new information came to light during the filming and one day Elisapee suggested that, in view of these discoveries, I should consider retelling the tale in print.

I demurred at first. After all, I had written two books about and around the subject. The first of these, *People of the Deer*, published in 1952, was a *cri du coeur* on behalf of the Ihalmiut, the last of whom were then living—and dying—in the Barren Lands of central Keewatin District.

It was also an account of their ancestral way of life and, especially, of their neglect and abuse by northern agents of government, by various commercial interests, and by missionaries—the combined results of which had amounted to something akin to unwitting genocide.

Not surprisingly the book came under furious assault from the established orders. Some claimed it was no more than a tissue of malicious falsehoods. Others, including the federal cabinet minister responsible for northern natives, insisted that the people I wrote about did not exist—had not *ever* existed, except in my imagination. So ferocious was the counter-attack from commerce, church, and state that echoes of it still reverberate and attempts are still being made to stigmatize me as a liar.

People of the Deer was followed eight years later by a second book, chronicling the further decline of the Ihalmiut. This one, *The Desperate People*, was partially concerned with documenting my earlier work but also included a detailed account of a new and ghastly calamity that took many Inuit lives and led to the virtual dissolution of the Ihalmiut.

[1] *Kikik* (Montreal: Words and Pictures Video/Video Mots et Images, 2000).

This time the critics chose a different tack. Faced with unassailable evidence of what had happened, most defenders of the bad old days ignored the book, doubtless hoping that in time it would be forgotten.

Their judgement turned out to be close to the mark. Forty years have passed since publication of *The Desperate People* (almost fifty since *People of the Deer*) and the world has forgotten what little it ever knew about the Ihalmiut. Bearing this in mind, I decided to accept Elisapee's challenge and tell the tale anew.

My principal reason for doing so is the same as that of writers who continue to tell the story of the Holocaust: to help ensure that man's inhumane acts are not expunged from memory, thereby easing the way for repetitions of such horrors.

But I had another reason for writing the present book.

In 1958, while travelling through Keewatin gathering accounts of the Kikik tragedy, I learned of an equally grievous catastrophe that had befallen another and related Inuit group. This calamity proved to be so dark and terrible that I forbore from including it in *The Desperate People* for fear a surfeit of horrors would cause readers to shut the book and turn their hearts and minds away. Now I am able to make amends for that omission.

About a quarter of this book's content concerns events previously depicted to some degree in *People of the Deer* and *The Desperate People*, but re-written with the addition of much new material. There may be some who will accuse me of self-plagiarism on this count, but I view what I have done as rescuing fading images from the erosion of time and have no apologies to make for that.

I do, however, apologize to my Inuit friends for not transposing Inuit names and words into the newly adopted standard orthography of Inuktitut. I have not done so because I wish to retain the flavour of the times when the events portrayed took place.

Thanks are due to the Hudson's Bay Company, the Royal Canadian Corps of Signals, the Territorial Court of the Northwest Territories, and the federal Department of Northern Affairs for access to their records.

My thanks go to many individuals, especially Elisapee Karetak, Ohoto, Owliktuk, Douglas Wilkinson, Richard Harrington, Ole Gjerstad, Alexander Lunan, Peter Lynn, Chesley Russel, Fr. Charles Choque, and Andrew Easton.

All major and most minor events described herein have been documented from official sources insofar as this was possible. Since this is not an academic tome, I have not provided a bibliography, but all the relevant materials can be readily found by anyone willing to undertake the search. *Tammarnit* (Mistakes), a scholarly examination of Inuit relocation in the eastern Arctic between 1939 and 1963, by Frank James Tester and Peter Kulchyski (UBC Press, Vancouver, 1994), contains an extensive bibliography, together with detailed notes dealing with the places, people, and times I have written about.

Most of the quoted conversations in my book were originally recorded on tape but have been edited in transcription and translation for clarity and brevity.

Farley Mowat
Brick Point, Nova Scotia, 2000

PART I

1 Northflight

The taxi driver waiting in front of Winnipeg's Fort Garry Hotel on a summer morning in 1958 was too enervated or too irritated by the heat wave incinerating southern Manitoba to open the car door. The best he could do was reach back and loosen the latch. I stuffed my sleeping bag and packsack onto the back seat and climbed in. It was only 7:00 a.m. but already the brazen prairie sun was turning the interior of the cab into a hotbox.

"Where ya wanna go?" the driver demanded aggressively.

"The float plane dock on the Red River, please. Know where it is?"

"Goddamn right I know. Why wouldn' I?" he snarled.

I tried to soften his mood by telling him I was a stranger in town, heading north. "To the Arctic coast. Maybe I'll meet the Ice Maiden, eh? And she'll cool me off?"

He was not to be placated. Wrenching at the wheel, he spun us out onto the parched pavement.

"Prob'ly get your balls froze off!" he snapped.

The float plane dock lay at the end of a rutted track plunging down the steep bank of the Red River. On this midsummer morning there was only one occupant: a high-shouldered, snub-nosed Beaver bush plane, freshly painted in silver and grey with a garish crimson tail and red stripes along her sides. She was perched on a pair of pontoons that looked big enough to float an airplane twice her size. Her name, CF-GQW, was writ large on her blunt wings.

A strapping big man wearing a flamboyant plaid shirt open almost to the navel greeted me as I hauled my gear down a flight of wooden stairs onto the floating dock. In his late thirties, he had an easy smile, a pencil-thin moustache, and a handshake to mash a marrow bone.

"Al Snyder. You'd be the writer fellow. I'm your jockey for this trip. Throw your stuff aboard. The boss'll be here any time, then it's away into the wild blue yonder."

A few months earlier I had been at home in southern Ontario when a rumour reached me that a group of Inuit calling themselves Ihalmiut, whom I had known in the Northwest Territories during the late 1940s, were in trouble.

The Ihalmiut had been the subject of my first book, *People of the Deer*, an impassioned plea on behalf of a people who had been harried to the verge of extinction. It was also a sometimes savage account of the treatment they had suffered at our hands.

I had been particularly scathing about northern agencies, including the Anglican Church; the Roman Catholic Church; the Royal Canadian Mounted Police; other arms of government; white trappers and free traders; and, last but not least, the Honourable Company of Gentlemen Adventurers trading into Hudson Bay, familiarly known as the Hudson's Bay Company. Stigmatizing these as the Old Empires of the North, I had accused them of bearing a heavy measure of responsibility for the disintegration of the lives of native peoples in general, but especially of the Inuit.

The counter-attack had been of epic proportions, but Pandora's box of northern horrors had been opened and there was no closing it thereafter. In the years following publication of *People of the Deer*, changes in the treatment of northern aborigines were proposed. Many of these were progressive. Some few were even implemented. By the end of 1956 I believed the frightful iniquities inflicted upon the Ihalmiut had become things of the past.

Although by the spring of 1958 disquieting whispers of a disaster in Ihalmiut country were taking on substance, I was inclined to discount them. The north is always awash with rumours and fearsome tales. In any case, I was by then deeply engaged in a book about Atlantic salvage ships and my mind was a long way from the Arctic.

Then came a letter from a government employee in the north reporting the violent deaths of several Ihalmiut whom I had known closely. Although much was obscure, it appeared that a hunter and shaman called Ootek had murdered his friend Halo and had then been killed by Halo's wife, Kikik. Moreover, this tragedy had occurred at the climax of an ordeal by starvation believed to have caused the deaths of many Inuit. My informant concluded with these words:

"Kikik survived and managed to save all her kids but one that froze to death. She's been arrested for murder. A lot of people are in a flap that the story will get out and blow sky high. What happened in Keewatin this winter is the worst mess I've ever seen in the north. You should look into it."

In April Kikik stood trial charged with the murder of Ootek and the death by neglect of her daughter. She was acquitted because the jury was *directed* to acquit her by a judge who unabashedly, and with scant regard for legality, sided with the Inuit.

Although I was by now being harassed by deadlines for my salvage book, I sent for transcripts of Kikik's trial. These contained only the bare bones of the story, and not all the bones. Clearly, much had been ignored—or suppressed. I could not turn my back on this affair. A call from Halifax to join a deep-sea tug on a rescue mission off Newfoundland gave me some breathing space, but on my return to Ontario I had to bite the bullet.

The only questions were how and when would I go north.

These were answered a few days later by a telephone call from Winnipeg.

When the caller introduced himself as Frank Walker, executive assistant to the Canadian Committee of the Hudson's Bay Company, I braced for trouble. Instead, I found myself being cordially invited to make an Arctic journey under the aegis of the foremost of the Old Empires of the North.

Walker, one of whose roles was public relations manager, explained:

"The head of our Arctic Division is about to head off on his annual inspection of trading posts in the central Arctic. He'll be travelling in our new Beaver and there's room for a passenger. You, Mr. Mowat, if you will. Food and lodging all found. You'd be gone about a month. How does it strike you?"

"Sounds interesting," I said cautiously. "Unless the plan is to dump me into the Arctic Ocean somewhere. What's all this in aid of, anyway?"

He laughed.

"Nothing special. Call it a goodwill gesture. You and the Company have been at odds too long. And, by the by, I apologize for the short notice. The fact is, the governors weren't all that thrilled when I suggested it might be nice to let bygones be bygones and offer you the trip. They came around. But of course not all the old hands think it's such a hot idea, extending the olive branch to you. Some of them think a dog whip might be more appropriate."

He laughed again.

"But don't worry. You'll be with Norman Ross. He's the Arctic manager and a gent of the old school. He'll see to it nobody takes it out of your hide."

Having been assured that the itinerary would include the key places I needed to visit if I was to discover what had happened to the Ihalmiut, I accepted the invitation. A week later I was standing by to board the Company's Beaver on the muddy Red River of the North.

Ross turned out to be a slightly built, middle-aged but athletic Scot with a gentle voice and manner. An Arctic veteran, he had joined the Company in Aberdeen in 1928 as an eighteen-year-old apprentice clerk and been sent to a remote outpost in Ungava Bay. Thereafter he had clerked at, then managed, trading posts at many places in the eastern Arctic. In 1954 he had been brought to the Canadian head office of the Hudson's Bay Company (HBC) in Winnipeg.

As manager of the Arctic Division, Norman Ross had become one of the grandees of the ancient Company. But acting the grandee was not his style.

Jauntily clad in grey trousers and a sporty checked jacket, he came nimbly down the stairs to join Al and me on the wharf. He looked more like a tennis player than a business executive burdened with great concerns. Yet he was embarking on a flight of several thousand miles across one of the last great wilderness regions left on earth, to visit and inspect more than two dozen trading posts, some of which were so remote as to be virtually unknown except to Indians and Inuit. By the time the Beaver returned Ross to Winnipeg, he would have flown over most of the continent's subarctic and Arctic region lying between Hudson Bay in the east and the Rocky Mountains in the west, and from timberline north to the coasts of the polar ocean.

Whatever he may have felt about being accompanied on this vast peregrination by one of the Honourable Company's most notorious critics, he played the perfect host.

"Take the co-pilot's seat, Mr. Mowat," he suggested as we prepared to clamber aboard. "I've paperwork to do, so I'll sit behind."

The Beaver rocked lightly, as if anxious to be off. We belted up. The engine fired. A local youngster, clearly consumed with eagerness to grow wings of his own, cast us off and with a rasping roar the plane charged down the river, climbed on her step, became airborne, and headed for Churchill some 650 miles distant to the north.

Built for cargo carrying, not for speed, a Beaver normally cruises about as fast as a car goes on a good highway. On this day we were not doing that well. Al passed me a set of headphones and flipped on the intercom.

"If you see birds passing us, don't fret. There's a bitch of a headwind. Going to be slow. But more fun than walking."

"Not as much fun as boating though." Norman's voice crackled in the phones. "The Company used to have its own little steamer on Lake Winnipeg. She'd take a week puttering along up to Norway House. Plenty of time to loll around and gab, usually with a bottle on the go. Now Al gets us there in four hours and you can't hear yourself think let alone have a decent talk. Progress, Mr. Mowat, is a two-edged sword." He switched off his microphone and retreated into his pile of papers.

Our course took us along the eastern coast of Lake Winnipeg, a body of water so vast as to deserve to be called an inland sea. We flew over what seemed to be interminable saffron-coloured beaches interspersed with sandy bays, lagoons, and rocky little coves—all backed by the dense greenery of virgin forests scarred here and there by old burns.

Within thirty minutes of take-off, we had virtually left man's handiworks behind us. The only evidence of human presence was a rare cluster of little shacks at the foot of some sheltered bay. Belonging to Icelandic fishermen from across the lake, these were occupied only during the summer months. We saw nothing of the fishermen or their boats. In fact, nothing made by man moved on the enormous expanse of open water stretching west and north to un-broken horizons.

Nevertheless, life abounded. GQW's noisy approach disturbed flotilla after flotilla of white pelicans, sending them lumbering over the cerulean surface of the lake like squadrons of prehistoric hydroplanes. As we passed Berens Island, we encountered half a hundred of them playing sailplane. With wings rigidly extended, they were soaring and circling in a thermal rising from the sun-warmed surface of the island. Although we were flying at three thousand feet, some pelicans had already gained so much altitude as to have become barely discernible snowflakes far above us.

Shortly thereafter, Al's jibe about being passed by birds came back to haunt him. Impelled either by curiosity or a wicked sense of humour, a bald eagle came plummeting down upon us. The big bird shot past so close I almost fancied I could hear the rush of air through its wings. Reacting like a fighter pilot, Al took evasive action.

The morning had been fine so far, but three hours into our flight a rampart of thunderstorms barred the way. Even from a distance they made a forbidding spectacle, flinging incandescent spears into earth and water. As we drew closer the turmoil became terrifying. I for one was very glad to make a landing at Norway House before the full fury of the gods fell upon us.

Norway House sits beside Playgreen Lake at the outlet of Lake Winnipeg. A fort was built here early in the nineteenth century, when the Company began extending its tentacles south and west from Hudson Bay. Not much remained of the four-square wooden fort except mounds of mouldering logs, an old gateway, and a collapsed powder magazine. The region's Swampy Crees now sold their furs and bought their goods at a miniature supermarket sporting plate-glass windows and a garish plywood facade with HBC painted large across its front.

Our visit was brief. While Norman did his business with the shy young manager of the new store, Al and I pumped gas from forty-five-gallon drums into the Beaver's capacious tanks—and warily watched the storm surging past to the east.

The three of us ate a belated lunch in a cozy little log café run by rotund Mrs. Lowe, widow of an old-time Company factor—as post managers were formerly called. She was incredulous to find the Company's Arctic commissioner not only eating at the same table with the notorious Farley Mowat but also sharing a nip of rum with the scoundrel. She showed her disapproval by pointedly serving me last and quickly whisking my plate away while offering second helpings of her exquisite moose stew and blueberry pie to Al and Norman. Hers was a demonstration of the kind of loyalty to "the old firm" that accounted in no small measure for the enduring success of the Company.

Airborne again, we followed a northeasterly course towards Churchill, still almost four hundred miles distant. Below us lay a wilderness of boreal forest mottled by uncountable lakes and riven by innumerable watercourses.

We had not gone far when the skies began closing down again. At first we were able to fly around and between the thunderheads, but eventually they became too numerous and close-ranked to be avoided. We flew right into one—and instantly GQW plummeted from fifteen hundred to two hundred feet. I now knew what falling down an elevator shaft must feel like.

Al brought the plane back to an even keel and we fled through a black pall at the base of the storm with lightning flaming close alongside. In pelting rain, and down to about a hundred feet, we scattered a flock of equally low-flying ducks and, by a mercy, hit none of them.

I was seriously frightened, but Norman seemed exhilarated. Leaning forward, he bellowed in my ear:

"... TOLD ME ... YOU'D BE A JONAH ... MAYBE LEAVE YOU ... CHURCHILL ..."

"*If* we get to Churchill," said Al on the intercom. He appeared to have lost his sunny optimism.

Conditions improved somewhat as we neared Split Lake, halfway to our destination. I was able to catch occasional glimpses of whitecaps on storm-lashed water, of wind-whipped black-spruce thickets, of sodden muskeg.

The respite was a brief one. Soon we were back in the toils of the storm gods. Niagaras of rain beat upon us, flailing against the thin aluminum skin of the cabin so fiercely the sound could be heard above the engine's roar. Al was apprehensive that the engine might drown. Later he told us that, uncertain of where we were, he had about made up his mind to land "on the next really damp patch" when, miraculously, the twin steel ribbons of the Hudson Bay Railway flashed into view under our pontoons.

Al instantly banked to follow the tracks, flying so low we could read the rain-streaked mile boards nailed to telegraph poles along the right of way. They told us we still had a hundred miles to go.

As the downpour and visibility grew worse, Al sounded as if he were talking to himself as much as to Ross and me.

"What the hell am I going to do if we meet a southbound train? Thank God there's no tunnels ... 'cause if there was we'd have to fly through them."

After what seemed like an interminable time we emerged from rain-blurred darkness. The sun began breaking through and GQW climbed back up into her accustomed element.

Below and around us lay a new world. The forest that had overlain the countryside like the pelt of some monstrous bear was now reduced to scabrous patches separated one from the other by ever-widening swaths of tundra.

This was timberline or, as the Chipewyans graphically term it, Land of Little Sticks. Constituting the border zone between the boreal forests and the tundra prairies that stretch north to the Arctic Ocean, it is a land so treeless that the first Europeans to see it named it the Barren Grounds.

While still twenty miles away, we glimpsed the high towers of Churchill's giant grain elevator gleaming in the pale sunshine. Beyond lay a measureless grey void: that northern mediterranean consisting of Hudson and James Bays and Foxe Basin that I call the Canadian Sea.

Norman was now in an expansive mood.

"Al, why don't you give Mr. Mowat an aerial tour of the Company's capital?"

Al nodded and banked westward to cross the mighty Churchill River a dozen miles inland from the coast. Then he flew downstream towards the great estuary at the river's mouth.

Ten miles long and five across, the estuary at low tide becomes a horrendous morass of mud and boulders through the middle of which the river threads its way to the sea. At high tide it is a shallow lake much favoured during the summer season by hundreds of belugas (white whales), who use it as a birthing place and nursery.

As we flew over it Norman, who was something of a history buff, provided a running commentary.

"See the rocky ridge jutting into the basin from the west? That's Old Fort, where the chap who discovered Churchill—a Dane called Jens Munk—tried to winter in 1619. He had two little ships—the *Lamprey* and the *Unicorn*—and sixty-five men. They planned to stake out a claim here for Denmark in the New World. By spring only Munk and two seamen were still alive. Scurvy killed the rest. Somehow those three managed to sail the *Lamprey* home. One try was enough for the Danes. They never came back."

GQW was now over the mouth of the estuary, where the snouts of two rocky coastal ridges approach one another leaving a gap through which the river debouches into Hudson Bay.

Near the terminus of the western ridge stood the ruins of a great star-shaped structure.

This was Fort Prince of Wales. Begun in the mid-seventeen hundreds, about a century after the HBC had established a post here to trade with Inuit from the north and Indians from the south and west, the fort had taken twenty years to build. It was supposedly the strongest stone fortification on the continent, but in 1782 a French naval squadron captured it without a shot being fired by either side.

Ross touched my shoulder and pointed east.

Fort Prince of Wales was dwarfed into insignificance by a mammoth concrete block a quarter-mile long and fifteen storeys high, towering above the basin's eastern point. The impact of this alien construct on a world of low-lying tundra was equal to that of an Egyptian pyramid thrusting out of the desert sands.

How had this monstrosity come into being? Norman knew the answer. In the mid-1920s a group of businessmen with access to the ear (and purse) of government conceived of a plan to create a mighty seaport on Hudson Bay, thereby shortening by as much as eighteen hundred miles the distance prairie grain then had to travel to reach Europe. Linked to southern Canada by rail, Churchill would become the chief shipping port, not only for prairie grain but also for western timber, minerals, and heaven alone knew what else. Furthermore, goods from the eastern hemisphere could travel to western Canada and the United States by the same route. Fabulous fortunes were to be made.

A railway between Winnipeg and Churchill was completed in 1929 at enormous cost. Nicknamed the Muskeg Special, it brought men and materials north to construct a port complete with piers, shipping services, and, not least, the elevator complex whose monolithic battery of immense concrete silos was intended to handle most of the grain grown in Manitoba, Saskatchewan, and Alberta. A grandiose town site was laid out on a stretch of gravel and perpetually frozen granite to the east of the estuary.

By 1932 the bulk of the work had been completed and those who had conceived of this colossal enterprise awaited their rewards.

Which never came.

For a variety of reasons (one being ice conditions that restricted commercial traffic in and out of Hudson Bay to about three months of the year), the dream of a great Arctic port dissolved even as had the dreams of avarice and glory that had led Jens Munk to Churchill three hundred years earlier—and that had built Fort Prince of Wales a century after that.

GQW banked to the southward over the settlement. We looked down upon a ragged assemblage of shacks, gimcrack wooden buildings, and abandoned railway sidings littered with rusty remnants of construction machinery. The sight was vaguely reminiscent of bombed towns I had seen in Europe during the war.

I recalled my previous visits to Churchill. The first had been in 1935 when, as a fourteen-year-old, I accompanied a great uncle who was an ardent ornithologist, to spend the summer searching for birds' nests on the tundra. At my then impressionable age Churchill had seemed a fascinating place inhabited by bearded trappers, intrepid fur traders, bronzed Chipewyan Indians, and fierce-looking sled dogs.

When I next saw it, in the early spring of 1946, Churchill had doubled in size but had lost whatever of romance it had once possessed. Scrofulous-looking sheds and shanties half-buried in winter drifts gave it the look of a set for a movie about a Siberian labour camp. The seaport-to-be had undergone a massive change when the war planted a sprawling military base on the tundra a few miles to the south. In consequence, the village had become the "recreation centre" (the *only* such resort within six hundred miles) for thousands of Canadian and U.S. troops undergoing Arctic training. Not to mince words, in 1946 it was a squalid slum whose citizenry seemed to consist largely of bootleggers, whores, and other camp followers.

As a battered taxi took us into town on the evening of our 1958 arrival, I had no expectations of finding things much improved. Which was just as well. Churchill seemed even shoddier and more dissolute than I remembered.

It did, however, have something for me. That evening in the beer parlour of the ramshackle Hudson Hotel, I encountered a man who was able and willing to tell me a good deal about the current situation of the Ihalmiut.

Bill Kerr had spent twenty-seven years in the Royal Canadian Mounted Police before being hired as a Northern Service Officer by the federal Department of Northern Affairs to assist in the rehabilitation of the Inuit living to the west of Hudson Bay. The Ihalmiut had been one of his chief concerns.

He was in a talkative mood that night. By the time I went to bed I knew the names of many of those I needed to contact and many of the places I needed to visit if I was to uncover the full story of what had happened to Kikik and the People of the Deer.

2 Eskimo Point

was as happy to leave Churchill as I had been to reach it. As a decrepit
taxi jounced us out to the little lake that served as a seaplane base,
thousands of waterfowl thronging the tundra ponds along the roadside

seemed to be urging us on our way.

Landing Lake harboured a flock of metal birds, including a Norseman (most famous of all bush planes), a Royal Canadian Air Force Otter (newest of the breed), an ante-bellum Fairchild, a little Cessna, and our trusty Beaver. Bobbing about on floats, they all seemed anxious to take to the air on this crystalline morning.

While we were topping up the Beaver's tanks, the Norseman bounded into the pale sky carrying five Grey Nuns to a Roman Catholic residential school at Chesterfield Inlet, three hundred miles to the north. Then the Air Force Otter thundered over the water laden with drums of fuel and crates of food for a lonely Department of Transport weather station at Ennadai Lake three hundred miles to the west. Next, the Cessna lifted off bearing a taciturn prospector in search of his pot of gold in the vast expanse of tundra to the northwest.

Finally it was our turn. Lightly laden, GQW rocketed off like a belated duck intent on rejoining its flock, but our "flock" had dispersed and we found ourselves alone in the cool morning air.

Al Snyder had been a bush pilot for ten years. Although his neatly clipped moustache gave him something of the appearance of a swashbuckler, he was in fact a cautious flier. "There are old pilots, and there are bold pilots, but there are no old, bold northern pilots" was one of his maxims.

He did, however, enjoy flying low.

"Higher you go, more boring it gets—and the farther there is to fall. I like to stay close to Mother Earth. That's where the action is."

We cruised at five hundred feet or thereabouts all the way to our first destination, Eskimo Point, a little community on the Hudson Bay coast halfway between Churchill and Chesterfield.

The tide was high so the coast was well defined, but at low tide the shore is fringed and obscured by several miles of muddy, rock-strewn flats. I knew about that, having tried to travel along it in an eighteen-foot canoe during an autumnal blizzard. Unable to reach dry land, which was so low as to be virtually invisible, my companion and I had been forced to spend most of a bitter night standing waist deep in frigid, breaking seas acting as living mooring posts to prevent the canoe from being blown across Hudson Bay.

This was a different sort of day. The sea was calm; the sky serene. The Barrens rolled into infinity to the west, a fluid palette of bog and muskeg greens and browns sponged into weird designs, flecked with innumerable lakes, and splintered by the quicksilver tracks of many rivers.

We were never short of places where GQW could have splashed down in case of need. The coastal plain appeared to consist as much of water as of land.

We overflew school after school of belugas. These giant Arctic porpoises seemed like smoky ghosts floating in the emerald waters of a shallow sea, wafting their way amongst massive clots of dark red kelp.

Fifty miles out of Churchill we crossed the sprawling mouth of Egg River. Here, on a little crescent beach between two rocky headlands, stood the long-abandoned HBC outpost of Nonala, its two little cabins storm-racked and wind-bleached.

Nonala had at one time been as far south as the Inuit of western Hudson Bay would venture. Scraggly little spruce copses marked it as being on the border of the forested regions that belonged by ancient tradition to the Chipewyan Indians.

An hour into the journey we flew over a skein of channels comprising the estuary of the Thlewiaza River. Big River, as it is locally known, was familiar to me. Looking down upon it, I vividly remembered how, accompanied by a young Metis named Charles Schweder, I had descended Big River at the conclusion of an eight-hundred-mile canoe trip through the interior of northern Manitoba and Keewatin.

Picking our way through the maze of estuary channels, Schweder and I had come upon the home of one of the last of the legendary Barren Lands trappers—a scattering of men who spent the better part of their lives in almost total isolation from what we refer to as the civilized world.

Born on the Labrador coast, George had drifted into the Arctic as a young fellow looking for adventure. For twenty years he had roamed the tundra, and it had made him one of its own. Eventually he had settled at the mouth of Big River in a rather luxurious cabin that he called his "tilt." During the winter he sallied far into the Barrens behind a magnificent team of huskies, trapping white foxes and wolves. In the summer he mostly stayed snugly at home, playing informal lord of the manor to the several families of Inuit who lived along the Thlewiaza.

We were George's guests for several days during which he fed us royally and tried to persuade us to winter with him, or at least to stay until after freeze-up, when he would be prepared to take us to Churchill by dog sled. The temptation was great, but we declined. Thereupon George gave us a precious drum of gas for our five-horsepower "kicker" and we were on our way.

Now George no longer lived on his river. Some said he had drifted south, or gone back to Labrador. Others thought that, knowing his time had come, he had gone into the country, Eskimo-style, to become an integral part of the world he had adopted. In any event, his tilt now stood empty to the winds.

The beach in front of it was occupied by a hodgepodge of wall tents, crates, nets, and sea-going canoes: a whaling camp established here two months earlier by the Department of Northern Affairs as part of a program to provide "gainful employment" for coastal Inuit. Six families were being paid one hundred dollars per month—very big money in that place and time—to net beluga. The carcasses of the little whales were supposed to be flensed, part of their blubber rendered into oil, and meat and blubber shipped to various distant Arctic communities to be used chiefly as dog feed.

As with so many bureaucratic decisions made at a distance, things had not worked out as planned. The mouth of the Thlewiaza is not a famous rendezvous for belugas. Although the hunters did eventually succeed in killing forty of a planned two hundred animals, most of these went to waste. There was no refrigeration, and the meat and blubber, packed in cellophane bags, soon rotted.

By the time we flew over the camp, putrid meat and blubber had turned the environs into those of a charnel house.

We were low enough to count half a dozen whale carcasses rolling in the tide. The few people in view waved in subdued fashion. Perhaps they envied us our ability to depart from that place so swiftly.

The clarity of the air was such that, when we were still thirty miles distant, we could see sunlight being reflected as by a heliograph from the tin roof of Eskimo Point's Roman Catholic church. Half an hour later we were over the long, sandy point itself.

The settlement was typical of those scattered along the coasts of the Far North. At its centre was the Hudson's Bay Company's spick and span compound, easily identifiable at a distance by its white-painted walls and garish red roofs.

Close to the "Bay" stood the Royal Canadian Mounted Police barracks, which included an office, a jail, and living quarters for a two-man detachment.

Somewhat more distant was the Roman Catholic mission brooded over by a squat and weather-worn church. An even smaller and shabbier church (hardly more than a chapel) represented the Anglican faith.

These were the hallmarks of the Old Empires of the North. For the rest, Eskimo Point consisted of a handful of shacks hammered out of packing crates and driftwood, together with fifteen or twenty grey and tattered tents.

GQW touched down on the calm waters of the harbour to find the Hudson's Bay Company freighter MV *Rupertsland* already at anchor there, having arrived the day before on her annual visit of resupply.

Her presence created pandemonium. A year's food, fuel, and general supplies had to be ferried ashore in landing craft, then carried by Inuit to the homes and warehouses of the white residents. Ship-time parties erupted ashore and afloat. Visitors from the ship included several RCMP officers heading for distant detachments, "Bay" officials, a dentist, and the Chief Medical Officer for the eastern Arctic. The latter pair seemed to be principally concerned with the needs of white patients but managed to find time to see some Inuit too.

There were even a few tourists, cameras at the ready to capture colourful images of Eskimos at work and at play. However, none of the visitors seemed to find their way to the Inuit tents, where they might have glimpsed the reality behind the stereotype of jolly little fur-clad people.

The ship's presence drew another notable visitor. A Stinson aircraft on floats came whining out of the north and pitched in the harbour. It was flown by a lanky, youngish man who tied up alongside our Beaver and introduced himself as the reverend Ledyard. No first name was offered. A soft southern accent hardly seemed to accord with his steely determination to save Eskimo souls—the Pentecostal way. It was his habit to descend on remote Inuit camps, load his small plane with children, then fly them to an indoctrination camp a few miles to the north of Eskimo Point. Here the children were subjected to intense proselytization for as much as a month before being returned to their parents. If not "saved" by then, they were presumably well on their way to redemption, American style.

There was a problem. Some Eskimo parents complained that their children had been taken away without their permission. Ledyard's response was that he had *God's* permission, an explanation that must have satisfied the RCMP since they declined to interfere.

Ross had planned to employ our Beaver for a few days ferrying supplies from *Rupertsland* to the outpost of Padlei, 120 miles inland to the northwest. I thought this would suit me admirably for Kerr had told me the surviving Ihalmiut were at Padlei. However, his information was behind the times. I had not been long at Eskimo Point before learning that the Ihalmiut were also there, having been transported to the settlement in March to await the government's pleasure as to their future disposition.

"They're camped just half a mile away," I was told, "but you'd best get the Mountie's okay before you go messing about with them. Corporal Gallagher—he's the boss cop—goes round the bend if anybody but him has anything to do with them."

Fortune seemed to be with me. Not only was Corporal Gallagher absent, but his second-in-command, a boyish constable from Nova Scotia, proved downright helpful.

"You don't need my permission to talk to those inland people. But I better warn you, they're in really poor shape. Even our local natives won't have much to do with them. Noah Gibbons, our native special constable, will go with you."[1]

Gibbons, a short and powerful man in his fifties whose father had been an American whaler, seemed uncomfortable about visiting the six grey and sombre tents where, after an interval of eleven years, I would again meet the Ihalmiut. He tried to prepare me by parroting his bosses' opinion that they were a lazy, worthless, and lawless lot. Noah was still expressing these sentiments when we arrived at the first of the canvas shelters.

The special constable called to the inmates in Inuktitut, ordering them out. There was a stir within and a man crawled into view, rising slowly and uncertainly to his feet, blinking against the brilliant sunlight. Dressed in torn and filthy remnants of cast-off army battle dress, he had the appearance of a soldier resurrected from the debris of some defeated army.

His name was Yaha. During my time amongst his people he had been a laughing man, big, vigorous, and full of *joie de vivre*.

There was no laughter in him now.

Yaha avoided looking at me. Neither did he look towards the beach behind us where the local Inuit had gathered to work as stevedores unloading *Rupertsland*'s barge as it came ashore. Mostly he stared at the ground, occasionally glancing inland into the rolling distance.

He replied monosyllabically when spoken to. Otherwise he seemed almost as immobile and uncomprehending as one of the *inuksuak*—the men of stone that stand on distant ridges across the Barren Grounds.

Suddenly Yaha ducked back inside his tent. Gibbons was embarrassed.

---

[1] I did not know it then, but soon after the Ihalmiut survivors were transported to Eskimo Point they were visited by Walter Rudnicki, an employee of the Department of Northern Affairs. He reported on their condition in these words:

"The last of the Ahearmiut [sic] are living in six igloos behind the policeman's house at Eskimo Point. They no longer have dogsleds, kayaks, or any of the accoutrements of life on the land. They no longer have any aim in life. Their existence is based on only one awareness—that they are now absolutely dependent on the white man."

"You see? His head gone bad. Better we go look some other tent."

The ambience in the other tents was no better. A few children showed some interest in my visit, but it was perfunctory. Howmik, widow of Ootek, crouched speechless under a filthy scrap of caribou hide, a crippled arm crooked around an eight-year-old daughter whose body was wasted by polio. In another tent old Hekwaw mumbled to himself while pointing to a herd of non-existent caribou. Shock-headed Miki came out of his tent to look me square in the eye, not with friendly recognition but with almost insensate hatred. Then he turned his back upon me.

Of them all only Owliktuk seemed reachable. Once a leader of his people, and still a handsome man, he gave me a half-smile and invited me to enter his tent. I could not face that. Dirt and stench did not repel me—it was the awareness that, once inside, I would be shut off from the world of neat white buildings, ships, airplanes—and living people.

So we sat outside on lichen-washed rocks and talked. Owliktuk's voice was low and listless, but he remembered everything that had taken place. He talked especially of the previous winter, which had seen the deaths of many men and women I had known. He spoke with a steady, monotonous insistence that was proof against the interruptions of my questions. His deeply lined face remained in repose, but it was the repose of a sleepwalker.

The spring within him unwound until gradually he fell silent. With a final effort he roused himself.

"He say," Gibbons translated slowly, "'Now you go 'way.' He say you no help his people. So better go. All the stuff he say makes me feel pretty bad. You know?"

So we came at last to the tent of Ohoto, the man who had been my closest friend amongst the people. When Ohoto failed to respond to the constable's summons, I pushed aside the hanging flap that shut the world away.

Ohoto was sitting in the centre of the floor space, legs extended straight before him, eyes cast down. He wore an ancient woollen sweater-coat caked with dirt and unravelled at sleeves and hem. Even when I squatted by his side and spoke his name, he gave no sign of being aware of my presence.

Gibbons again apologized.

"He don't see or hear good. Got hurt once, got an eye smashed. You got to yell at him."

I touched Ohoto's arm instead. Still there was no reaction. Looking beyond him in the dimness I saw his wife, Nanuk, whom I did *not* recognize. She who had been a tubby, smooth-faced, and jovial matron when I last saw her was now a gargoyle, grotesquely bent and almost devoid of the mane of gleaming ebony hair that had distinguished her. Suckling a scrawny infant, she stared soundlessly back at me with eyes as flat and black as iron slugs.

Slowly Ohoto raised his head. For a moment his one good eye searched my face.

"Skibbee?" he asked, thick lips parting in a grin of recognition.

Ohoto's use of this Inuit adaptation of my old nickname—Squib— lightened the gloom. In other days he had delighted to play the clown; now some vestige of those days returned. He reminded me of the time he had pretended to arrange a marriage for me with an ancient aunt of his. And of the mirth that had overwhelmed everyone but me as the old lady offered herself, and I rejected her advances while struggling to retain some remnants of dignity.

For my part, I reminded Ohoto of some of his attempts to transform himself into a *kablunak* (a white man), including making a toothbrush out of wolf bristles and using it with sand instead of toothpowder. Fortunately, I had caught him at this before he had been able to damage his huge white teeth irreparably.

But after a while Ohoto stopped speaking. Or listening. His gaze dropped until he was again staring blankly at the dirty floor.

He had gone from me.

3 Ennadai

Tradition has it that the first-footers in the treeless lands of
northern Canada were musk ox and reindeer hunters working
their way eastward from Asia. Thousands of years ago they found

what they sought in a vast triangular tract of Canadian Arctic whose apex points to the Mackenzie River delta, and whose base stretches nine hundred miles northward from Churchill on Hudson Bay to Fury and Hecla Strait separating the continental mainland from the Arctic islands.

Encompassing more than a million square miles, this enormous swath of tundra became home to a multitude of Inuit who knew nothing of seals and the sea. An inland people, their lives were predicated on the comings and goings of almost inconceivably huge herds of caribou.

They were a fortunate people. Although the European invasion of North America that began in the seventeenth century devastated the lives of natives almost everywhere else on the continent, the people of the Arctic prairies remained largely unaffected until near the end of the nineteenth century.

They were not a nation, nor even a tribe, but a loose association of groups consisting of up to a dozen families. All were, however, united in their allegiance to *Tuktu*—the caribou—which, in their millions, not only furnished the necessities of life but most of whatever else these people needed. Caribou skins provided clothing (the warmest and lightest known), footwear, tents, sleeping robes, coverings for kayaks, even the heads of drums. *Tuktu* gave people meat, and fat both to eat and to fill their lamps; sinews for sewing; and antler and bone for the manufacture of innumerable hunting and domestic implements, even including children's toys. *Tuktu* was life itself to human dwellers in the Barren Lands.

Early in the twentieth century arctic fox fur became extremely fashionable in Europe and the United States. By 1910 the exquisitely silky-white (or sometimes silvery-blue) pelage of an arctic fox was worth as much as fifty dollars in the New York market.

As a result, the country that the first Europeans had named the Barren Lands was no longer viewed as a useless desolation. It became the focus of a white-gold rush. This brought turmoil and disruption into the lives of the caribou people and resulted in a series of disasters that shattered their delicately balanced way of life.

By 1924 traders had reached the southern borders of the Arctic prairies near Ennadai Lake, where they made contact with an extremely isolated group of inland Inuit calling themselves Ihalmiut. At Ennadai, as elsewhere across the Barrens, the old verities of life began eroding as fox took pride of place over caribou. Good fox-trapping grounds and proximity to a trading post came more and more to determine where, and how, people lived. Spears, bows and arrows, and traditional hunting methods were discarded in favour of repeating rifles.

A pitiless butchery ensued. By the late 1920s caribou slaughter had become a bloodletting on an unprecedented scale, not only on the tundra, but also to the south inside timber where the deer (as caribou are generally known throughout the Far North) mostly wintered and where Indians and white trappers alike butchered them by the tens of thousands.

Then came 1929 and the Great Depression. The profits to be made from white fox pelts collapsed catastrophically and by the early 1930s most traders had abandoned the interior plains. The people of the plains, conditioned to dependence on trade goods, now found themselves deprived of guns, ammunition, flour, lard, and other things that had become virtual necessities. To make matters worse, the deer were in decline.

The rest of that decade saw recurrent famine years. When, in 1940, the Hudson's Bay Company closed its outpost in the southern Barrens, only 138 Ihalmiut (there had once been several times that number) remained alive.

Deprived of ammunition for their few serviceable rifles, they reverted as best they could to traditional hunting methods such as spearing caribou from kayaks at river crossings. And so they managed to endure until the autumn of 1942, when they missed the southbound caribou migration.

Nobody knows why the shrunken herds failed to follow their ancestral paths that year, but fail they did. During the following winter forty-four Ihalmiut starved to death.

The fearful magnitude and dreadful details of what ensued during the next several years are reported in *People of the Deer*, so need not be repeated here. Suffice it to say that by the spring of 1947 only forty-nine Ihalmiut remained alive.

I first arrived in the Ihalmiut lands in May of 1947. Accompanied by Charles Schweder, a young Metis, I spent the next several months travelling in the country. An early encounter with the Ihalmiut was at their caribou-skin tents pitched on the shores of a group of little lakes close to Ennadai and the headwaters of the Kazan River.

The first tent I visited belonged to Ohoto and his wife, Nanuk. Ohoto was then about thirty-five, squat and powerful, with the rolling gait and enduring energy of a bear. A mercurial man of wit, he was usually jovial, though subject to occasional moods of despondency. He had fathered three children, all of whom had died at an early age of starvation or disease. Now Nanuk was pregnant once again.

Ootek's tent was not far away. Of an age with Ohoto, Ootek was a mystic and a shaman. He lived with his wife, Howmik, and their five-month-old daughter, Kalak, who had been born deaf and dumb as a consequence of the last famine. She was the sole survivor of three children born to this couple.

Ootek's closest comrade was Halo, who lived nearby with his wife, Kikik, and their two surviving children.

Sharp-featured Owliktuk had pitched his tent on the shore of another of the Little Lakes in company with big, good-natured Yaha. They shared this lake with Miki, a taciturn and cautious younger man whose father, a white trapper, had abandoned Miki and his mother one singularly bitter winter.

The families of Pommela, Onekwaw, Katelo, and Alekahaw were camped beside yet another of the Little Lakes.

These were the Ihalmiut.

In the spring of 1948 I returned to their country in company with biologist Andrew Lawrie, nominally to study caribou. I renewed my friendship with the People of the Deer, especially Ohoto, with whom Lawrie and I travelled through what had once been the heartland of Ihalmiut country.

When, in the autumn of that year, the caribou herds drifted south into the forests where they would spend the winter, I prepared to follow. My winter base would be on Reindeer Lake in northern Manitoba, some two hundred miles to the south of Ennadai.

Ohoto and a young man named Mounik were at hand to see me off. Since there is no word for "goodbye" in Inuktitut, they simply waved as I clambered aboard the float plane. I shouted that I would be back in the spring when the deer returned to the Arctic plains. None of us could foresee that ten years would elapse before we would meet again.

Although I failed to return in 1949, Ennadai did receive visitors from the outside world that year.

On December 28, 1948, a column of mechanical behemoths clanked and rumbled out of Churchill heading north and west into the frozen plains. The column consisted of eight giant Caterpillar tractors towing sleds of fifteen tons' capacity, laden with construction materials. Their objective was Ennadai Lake, three hundred air miles to the northwest.

This strange armada voyaged across a sea of snow and ice for forty days and nights. The days were short, the nights long, and the cold almost intolerable, sometimes dropping to fifty degrees below zero. Breakdowns were frequent and repairs an agony. Nevertheless, on February 4, 1949, the tractor train came to a halt on the snow-shrouded shore of an arm of Ennadai Lake, a scant day's journey from the snow houses of the Ihalmiut. It took only a short time to unload the sleds and then the tractors rumbled eastward out of the Barrens.

It was not until mid-July that the ice loosened its grip on the eastern arm of Ennadai Lake. Shortly thereafter a Royal Canadian Air Force flying boat descended heavily upon those frigid waters. Taxiing to a sandy stretch of beach near the vast array of crates and containers left by the tractor train, the Canso disgorged a ten-man construction crew. The big plane made several more trips in succeeding days, bringing in more men and materials for the construction of yet another link in a web of electronic surveillance being spread across the Arctic as part of the Cold War.

As July passed into August, the piles of material at Ennadai were transformed into buildings and high steel towers. One late August day, diesel generators began to thunder. The non-commissioned officer in charge of a detachment of the Royal Canadian Corps of Signals manning the station turned on his transmitter and contact was established with the modern world.

A few days later contact was established with a different and much older world.

Six men clad in skin clothing breasted a ridge behind the station and looked down upon the strange buildings, the high towers, massive stacks of supplies, piles of fuel-oil barrels, and a yellow bulldozer snorting like a wounded musk ox as it worked on what would become an aircraft landing strip.

Led by Ohoto, the visitors came slowly down the slope. White men suspended work to stare at these beings who seemed to have sprung out of some distant time. The whites were at a loss to know how to act, but Ohoto knew the form. He ambled forward, seized Corporal McIsaac's hand, and shook it with such gusto that the soldier pulled away in alarm.

It was a memorable moment for all concerned, especially for the corporal, who wrote:

"I felt a bit like Columbus when he laid eyes on his first Indian. Only two of my gang had ever even seen an Eskimo before. They sure were a curious-looking bunch."

So began a relationship that was to endure in one form or another for seven years.

In October 1949, Corporal McIsaac added:

"The local Eskimos have taken a great proprietary interest in our welfare, regarding us as a feckless crew who need looking after. After first snowfall Ohoto paid a visit, took our measurements with a length of string, and later brought back complete suits of caribou clothing for us, including mittens and skin boots."

Having outfitted the newcomers with proper winter gear, the Ihalmiut continued to help them adjust to, and survive in, a fiercely unfamiliar land. In January 1950, the bulldozer broke down and the airstrip could not be cleared of snow to allow a Dakota transport carrying urgently needed fuel oil to land. The station was about to shut down for want of heat and electricity when Ohoto mustered the Ihalmiut and led them to the airstrip. It took the Inuit three days of hard shovelling in blizzard conditions to clear the runway, but on January 25 the Dakota was able to land and the situation was saved.

Inuit and soldiers provided mutual assistance and got along famously. Ohoto's penchant for practical jokes, and his bawdy wit, especially appealed to the soldiers, one of whom referred to him in a letter as "the Eskimos chief clown and funny guy. We're thinking of adopting him into our outfit just for laughs."

Ohoto would have been delighted had they done so. During the last agonizing years, he had begun to believe that the best hope for the ongoing survival of himself and his people was to abandon their past and somehow transform themselves into *kablunait.*

Noblesse oblige was the order of the day. In the autumn of 1949, the non-commissioned officer in charge of the station radioed the civil authorities at Churchill that ammunition was urgently needed or the Ihalmiut might be unable to make an autumnal caribou hunt. However, the only (and long-delayed) response was a message from the NCO's own superiors instructing him not to concern himself with matters that were the responsibility of the RCMP and other federal authorities. The soldiers had been effectively told to mind their own business.

This they found hard to do. During the winter of 1949–50 a lack of caribou and of ammunition combined to bring famine to most of the inland people. The Ihalmiut were lucky. Although at least thirty Inuit starved to death in other parts of Keewatin, the Ennadai people survived because the soldiers shared their rations with them.

The calamity in Keewatin that winter may have had something to do with Ottawa's subsequent decision to put the Ihalmiut under "the protection" of a pair of ex-trappers who were starting a commercial fishing business in northern Manitoba and who needed labour.

Early in April 1950, a policeman in a ski-equipped Otter flew to Ennadai and conducted what was, in effect, a forced deportation.

Carrying little more than the clothing in which they stood, the Ihalmiut were flown in several relays to the south end of Nueltin Lake, well within forested country. Here they were left to become fisher folk. The fact that they had neither nets nor boats seems not to have troubled the authorities, who may have presumed the fish company entrepreneurs would provide the requisite equipment. This they never did.[1]

Disoriented, fearful of the surrounding forests and of the Indians who inhabited them, and without any real means of making a living, the Ihalmiut sank into a kind of torpor from which they roused themselves only when one of their young women died in mysterious circumstances—possibly murdered.

The Ihalmiut fled. They walked home. It took five weeks for men, women, and children to traverse a distance of only about 150 air miles. Their journey entailed travelling more than twice that distance over some of the roughest country in Keewatin, around innumerable lakes, and across scores of rivers. The Israelites fleeing from Egypt had no greater difficulties to overcome. But in due course the Ihalmiut arrived back at the Little Lakes near Ennadai, where they began trying to reconstruct their lives.

Having lost much of their gear, they were unable to make adequate preparations for the coming winter. Indeed, all that saved them from famine was the presence of the weather station staff, from whom they received food enough to keep them alive until spring.

The events of that winter established a debilitating pattern. During succeeding years the Ihalmiut became increasingly reliant upon the weather station. From being a self-sustaining people they were insensibly transformed into a people of the dole.

Frequently suffering from periods of malnutrition often verging on famine, they endured. But at heavy cost. Sickness became almost endemic. During the spring of 1954 influenza and mumps swept through the camps, infecting almost everyone.

---

[1] Touted as a winter fishery that would deliver frozen fish by air to the railhead at Churchill two hundred miles away, the scheme had no prospects of success and was abandoned.

Ohoto was especially afflicted by this new visitation. His wife, Nanuk, a widow five years his senior, had seen two husbands and all but one of her previous children, a daughter called Ilupalee, die of disease or starvation. Now she was pregnant and she and Ohoto desperately hoped the child would be a son.

In May Nanuk collapsed with mumps, or influenza, or both. The soldiers were able to ship her out to Churchill aboard a military plane. There she gave birth to the much-desired son. He was stillborn. The doctors concluded his death was due to acute toxemia in the mother brought about by prolonged malnutrition.

The situation at Ennadai was grim that summer. The soldiers found themselves increasingly beleaguered by sick and hungry people. No relief was sent until mid-August, when the authorities flew in twelve hundred pounds of half-rotten meat. The shipment elicited this radio message from the sergeant in charge of the station to his superiors.

ONE AIRCRAFT LOAD OF CONDEMNED MEAT SENT HERE BY DEPT RESOURCES AND NORTHERN DEVELOPMENT FOR STARVING ESKIMOS STOP THIS IS THE FIRST MEAT TRIBE HAS TASTED FOR MONTHS STOP CONDITION OF PEOPLE PARTICULARLY CHILDREN IS PITIFUL MAIN DIET FLOUR AND A FEW FISH STOP DOGS ARE JUST BAGS OF BONES AND HAIR AND HAVE BEEN TURNED LOOSE TO FEND FOR THEMSELVES STOP ALL OLD BONES CARIBOU HOOVES IN AREA HAVE BEEN GATHERED BY ESKIMOS TO MAKE SOUP STOP THE GENERAL HEALTH IS POOR AND THEY ARE CATCHING ALL SORTS OF DISEASE STOP TO DATE TWELVE ESKIMOS EVACUATED TO CHURCHILL FOR HOSPITALIZATION

Through seven years the soldiers had done what they could to help the Ihalmiut. In September of 1954 that relationship ended when responsibility for operating the station was transferred to the federal Department of Transport, and the soldiers were replaced by civilians.

That autumn the Department of Northern Development, which was responsible for the Inuit, shipped in sufficient ammunition to enable the Ihalmiut to make a hunt. Although the multitudes of deer seen in past years did not appear, enough were killed to meet food and clothing needs. There was even sufficient meat to keep the dogs vigorous and to allow the men to range far out over the plains trapping foxes. This they did with such success that in January 1955, Ohoto, Ootek, Halo, and Owliktuk were able to undertake the long sled journey to the nearest trader, an HBC outpost at Padlei, 170 air miles northeast of Ennadai and 100 inland from the bay coast.

The travellers were welcomed by their cousins, the Padleiermiut, in traditional fashion with drum-dances and song-feasts. Then the visitors went to the post, where they traded pelts for tea, tobacco, duffle cloth, and whatever else was needed. As they drove their sleds back to the Little Lakes, they were contented men.

The Ihalmiut were not alone in their good fortune that winter. At Padlei, along the Thelon, at Baker Lake, and even on the distant Back River, Inuit witnessed the apparent resurgence of caribou numbers with hope reborn.

Their hope was to be short-lived. The spring of 1955 saw only a trickle of caribou at the usual hunting places. People got by that summer on fish, birds, ground squirrels, and berries, but over them loomed the dread that *Tuktu* might fail them in the fall.

This was the summer the Ihalmiut were "discovered." The Reverend Ledyard from the U.S.-based Northern Evangelical Mission to the Eskimos flew a small plane to the Little Lakes, where he loaded three children aboard and carried them off to a Bible camp near Eskimo Point to be indoctrinated with Christian values. According to Ohoto and others, this was done without the consent of the parents.

Then came a Dutch anthropologist employed by the federal government to "investigate the legal structure of Ihalmiut society." In his report he offered suggestions for the ongoing treatment of the inland people, amongst which was this gem:

"Only a close teaching of the gospel will save their small communities and offer some perspective for the future. It needs no elucidation that the conditions for personal happiness can be assured by this."

The fact of the Ihalmiuts' existence (something government spokesmen had categorically denied at the time *People of the Deer* was published) was confirmed on August 13 when photographers and writers from *Life* magazine flew to Ennadai. They came to do a story on

Stone Age people in the modern world. In February of 1956 twenty-one-year-old Mounik, his fifteen-year-old wife, Ookanak, and their baby son, Tabluk, appeared on the cover of *Life* above the banner title "Stone Age Survivors."

Fame had found the Ihalmiut, but so, yet again, had famine. Bill Kerr, one of the Northern Service officers recently hired by the Department of Northern Affairs, reported: "The caribou hunt at Ennadai in the fall of 1955 was just short of a total failure." In the event, the people obtained only enough meat to last until November. Thereafter they again found themselves dependent on the weather station.

However, things had changed since the departure of the soldiers. The new civilian employees were, by and large, hostile to the Ihalmiut, whom one of them categorized as "a filthy, stinking bunch who don't want to work for a living ... bums who foul up the place." When the staff were instructed by the RCMP to keep the natives away from the station as much as possible, they were happy to comply, although, according to the Ihalmiut, there were some significant exceptions.

Interviewed in 1999, Mounik recalled:

"The first white men that came [to Ennadai], the soldiers, were real good. They sent sick people to be treated down south. We could trade fox pelts with them for food and shells. The other white men [civilian employees of the Department of Transport] started using our women. And when we [men] would go there to try to trade fox pelts, they would just tell us go away."[1]

To which his wife, Ookanak, added:

"Us women were being used. If we didn't go they would mistreat us. I know this very well because I am a woman and I have experienced it. The women loved their children, so they would bring themselves to the white men in order to get something to eat, to feed their children."

---

[1] In the summer of 1999, while engaged in making his film about the Kikik tragedy, producer Ole Gjerstad flew a number of the Ihalmiut back to visit their ancestral home at Ennadai. The group included three of Kikik's children, together with Mounik and Ookanak, who were by then the only surviving elders. The occasion opened the floodgates of memory for them.

When Ohoto visited the station hoping to obtain medical help for Nanuk, who by then was barely able to move, his plea was ignored. It seems to have been at this juncture that Ohoto turned his back on the *kablunait* and what they represented. No longer would he try to become one of them.

Rations doled out to the Ihalmiut that winter were sufficient to keep body and soul together.[1] Nobody died. Nevertheless, by March of 1956 the people were about as close to physical and psychic exhaustion as they could come and still survive.

In the middle of that month they were visited by a senior official of DNA. After peering into some of their tent shelters, he concluded the people lacked almost everything a human being needed in that hard land, including sufficient clothing and bedding. The Ihalmiut, he reported, were suffering so severely from malnutrition they were no longer able to fend for themselves. Or for their dogs. Of seventy-five dogs alive at the beginning of winter, only five skeletal survivors could still be found.

Shocked by this first-hand warning of another disaster in the making, the Ottawa mandarins agreed that steps must be taken. But what steps? The solution ultimately adopted originated with Corporal Gallagher, in charge of the RCMP post at Eskimo Point. Gallagher's proposal was supported by Henry Voisey, manager of Padlei Post, and by Bill Kerr, Northern Service Officer for the region.

The plan called for yet another removal of the Ihalmiut: this time to the Padlei region where they would be supervised by the police and Voisey "while recovering their ability to live off the land."

The decision to exile them once again was taken in August 1956, but was not implemented until a year later. The winter of 1956–57 became a repeat of the previous one.

---

[1] Food, ammunition, and other supplies sent to the Ihalmiut were *not* a charge against government. They were mostly paid for from Family Allowances due every Canadian, from wages owed the Inuit by the weather station, or from the sale of fox pelts trapped by the Ihalmiut. Although these funds belonged to the people, they were administered by the RCMP, the HBC, and the Northern Service Officers.

In April 1957, Canon Sperry of the Anglican Church was forced down at Ennadai by weather during a flight from Churchill to Yellowknife. He was appalled by what he saw.

"There was a group of about fifty Eskimos. ... They presented a picture of such abject misery and such indescribable filth that I found it hard to believe they were Eskimos at all. They stood huddled in old skins, were gaunt and dirty ... faces hollowed out by malnutrition. Between the fifty of them they had one dog, if it could be described as such. I visited their hovels, circular walls of snow with old skins forming a roof. ... That morning, they said, they had breakfasted on pieces of old caribou skin, boiled. This meagre starvation diet was supplemented by the leavings of the radio men at the nearby station. Indeed, they formed a pitiable spectacle."

Barely a month later the Ottawa authorities initiated what they hoped would be the ultimate solution to the problem posed by the Ihalmiut.

4 The Exiles

On the morning of May 10 an RCMP Otter circled the Ennadai station. The snarl of its radial engine brought people out of the seven tents pitched half a mile from the buildings. As they watched the Otter glide in for a landing, they also became aware of the blatting rumble of the station's bulldozer climbing the slope towards their camp.

Here is how Mounik remembered that scene.

"All of a sudden the tractor come right by our tent. I thought they come to pick me up because sometimes I worked with the tractor. He stopped right by our tent and looked in and told us to leave. I was wondering, what is he doing? What does he want? He told us to go to the plane. While we were walking we looked back and see the tractor drive over the tents, wrecking our belongings. There was nothing left, so we kept on walking. A policeman had a stick in his hand, pointing at us, telling us to go to the plane. He was scary, so we followed his orders. They didn't explain. We didn't know what was going on. We didn't take any of our stuff, only three dogs. The tractor drove back and forth over our things while we got on the plane."

Here is Ookanak looking at the pile of stone and gravel where the Ihalmiut tents had stood some forty years earlier.

"Right here is where our belongings were buried. ... Look, an old rag from the tent! Look, there should be some [caribou] bones, but everything has been buried! Right here is where our belongings were buried. ... We were starving then. My only child, Tabluk, I couldn't feed him. He tried to suck but instead of milk there was blood coming out. We had nothing to eat. This is what I've always remembered from the bottom of my heart. I will never forget this. ... This is where our tent was."

On that day of removal in 1957, stone *inuksuak*, "semblances of men" erected by past generations of Inuit on the surrounding hills, watched with sightless eyes as the last of the Ihalmiut were herded into the aircraft.

It required five flights to transport the fifty-seven survivors to their new place of exile. Again they were allowed to take nothing with them except what they could carry in their hands and on their backs. Traps, sleds, kayaks, two canoes, tents, and other heavy gear had to be abandoned. The police were in such a hurry that when Ohoto asked permission to run to a nearby cache and fetch a rifle, he was refused. "Maybe they think I run away and hide," he said afterwards.

Maybe they did.

The police told the deportees they were being moved for their own good to a better country. The Ihalmiut did not believe it. They were convinced then, and have never changed their minds, that they were moved at the insistence, and for the convenience, of the white men who ran the weather station.

Here is Mounik:

"They did not want us around there. We don't know why. All we did was bring fox pelts for them to send away to be traded for food and other things we needed. That was all we asked of them.

"Why did they come here anyway? We lived here way long before them. They invited themselves to our land. We didn't ask them to come. We didn't say 'Come to us. Help us.' Ihalmiut always had camps here. Then they came and began building houses and later they started telling us to move farther and farther away. Why? We never bothered them until we started to starve. I think now if we had always kept away from them we would not have been moved to a country different from our own."

And Ookanak:

"I don't like what they did. I ask myself why they kick us out of our home. They don't even live there now.[1] No one is there. ... It hurts to remember, but I don't hate them or anything, [although] it bothered me for a long time. It bothered me, because we were *not* beggars. We were Ihalmiut. We were *people!*"

The transportation to the shores of Offedal Lake (part of Henik Lake), 50 air miles to the west of Padlei Post and 150 from Eskimo Point, was completed on May 11. The Ihalmiut were then given new tents and some food and left to their own devices. They had only three dogs, no kayaks or canoes, no sleds, and so no means of going anywhere except on foot. This may not have been a planning oversight. It may have been done deliberately to make it difficult for them to return to their old home. Even as the bulldozing of their Ennadai camp would have discouraged any attempt to return to it.

[1] The station at Ennadai was abandoned in the 1970s and has stood empty ever since, gradually succumbing to wind and weather.

When I talked to him in 1958, Owliktuk vividly remembered what life in the Promised Land had been like during the weeks after the transportation.

"We surprised when the police told us this was good country they bringing us to. It was hungry country. The food they left only lasted a few days.

"We went looking for deer trails and crossing places. We found none so we knew no deer had been here for a long time. There was lots of wood, so we had fires, but little to cook. There were a few ptarmigan. We tried fishing but when we had cut through many feet of ice our jiggers caught nothing.

"One day we heard airplanes to the southwest and thought they were landing. Anoteelik and Mounik went that way and found some whitemen camped by the side of a big lake. Next day most of us men went to that place and the whitemen gave us a little food. It was very little. Not enough to help everyone.

"Pommela, the *angeokok* [shaman], had been too weak to go to the whiteman's camp. The people in his tent were starving and he could no longer do anything to help them, so he went walking on the land and was gone from us.

"Some of us went back to the whitemen then and told them what was happening. They had a radio and they said they would send a message we were hungry and some food would be brought. Nothing happen for a long time. We had little strength and mostly stay in the tents. We wish we had run away from Ennadai when the police came to bring us here."

The planes the Ihalmiut had heard were flying building materials to Bray Lake, southwest of Offedal, with which to construct a prospecting base for the Sherritt Gordon mining company. One of the party employed building the camp was a young man named Peter Lynn. He was among the first to encounter the Ihalmiut. He wrote to me:

"I learned from Ohoto, who could speak a few words of English, that the group was starving and already one of their elder tribesmen had died.

"A few days later an old Eskimo woman with a child came to my tent. [This was Ohoto's wife, Nanuk, who was then just forty-one years of age.] I gave them a sack of flour, 30 pounds. The old woman's eyes were in poor shape, red-rimmed and almost completely swollen shut."

On May 17 Lynn, guided by Anoteelik, visited the Ihalmiut camp.

"The walk took about six hours. We arrived on the shore of a small lake and I could see eight or nine tents in a huddle near a grove of small spruces, some of which had been cut down. I asked Anoteelik about this and he said the people had taken the bark and boiled it, then drank the liquid and ate the bark. I tried some and immediately retched up this bitter substance.

"I saw no food whatever except the sack of flour I gave the old lady some days earlier. The women were making a kind of biscuit out of this and giving it to the children and to the men still strong enough to go hunting.

"Near the end of June the construction job was finished and we prepared to leave. All the perishable food—it wasn't much—we gave to the Eskimos. Canned and boxed food-stuffs were piled in one of the aluminum huts we had built. This was to be used by the prospecting crews who would come in after break-up.

"Ohoto again tried to impress the seriousness of the situation on me. He said, 'What shall we do? We are hungry and in there is food. If we starve we will have to take the food.'

"I mentioned this to the foreman but he could not accept the responsibility of giving Company food to the Eskimos. I thought once we got to Churchill everything would be all right for the RCMP would immediately handle the situation once they were aware of it. I told Anoteelik and Ohoto I would inform the RCMP. [This I did] only to be curtly informed that the RCMP were quite aware of the circumstances of these people and sent in an aircraft periodically to check on these people. There was nothing to worry about, and these people were being looked after."

On June 5 Bill Kerr, the regional NSO stationed at Churchill, made a quick stop at Offedal during a flying visit to Padlei. By then the

Ihalmiut had split into two camps. Kerr visited only the smaller one, which consisted of four families. It was late in the day and the aircraft was due back at Churchill before dark, so Kerr unloaded some Family Allowance supplies and departed. Later he was to say he had relied on assurances from the RCMP that the situation in which the Ihalmiut found themselves was not serious.

The families in the second camp did what they could to save themselves. In order to be able to spear caribou in the water—if and when any appeared—Owliktuk built a kayak of spruce covered with canvas from his tent.

The caribou did not come. Neither did the police. The only food obtainable was the occasional hare, a few ptarmigan, a very few fish—and the bark of spruce trees. By mid-June the situation had become desperate.

Nanuk was again pregnant and Ohoto knew that unless food was soon found for her the unborn child would probably die. So one June day he took matters into his own hands. Accompanied by Mounik and a man named Iootna, Ohoto led the way to the prospectors' base at Bray Lake. It was a long, hard trek. The spring thaw forced the hunger-weakened men to wade waist-deep through frigid meltwater streams and to make long detours around ponds and lakes on which ice was turning black and mushy. They persevered because they had no choice.

In mid-July, when the inland lakes were free of ice, Sherritt Gordon's prospectors flew in to their new Bray Lake base. They found the door of the stores building ajar and some food missing. A day later a figure appeared over a nearby ridge. It was Ohoto, who had heard the plane arriving and had come to explain what had happened.

Perhaps because he possessed only a little English, or perhaps because the white men were angry, Ohoto's explanation was rejected and he was chased away. The prospectors radioed Churchill reporting the theft.

If the police had been slow to respond to reports of starvation in the Ihalmiut camps, they made up for it by the alacrity with which they acted when lawbreaking was involved. A few days later the RCMP Otter flew

Corporal Gallagher to Offedal. The malefactors were arrested and taken to Eskimo Point, leaving their wives and families largely dependent upon what help the remaining people in the camps could give them.

Punishment of the accused began two months before their trial when the police put the three men to work breaking rocks into gravel for the paths around the detachment building.

It was not long before a stone chip flew into Ohoto's right eye and ruptured it. He was given first aid, but the wound became infected. Two weeks later Corporal Gallagher shipped Ohoto off to Churchill for medical attention. The report that accompanied him blamed the patient for aggravating the injury "by rubbing it." Nothing was said about its initial cause.

On arrival in Churchill's transit camp for natives, Ohoto was sent to the local hospital. The staff there declined to admit him and he was returned to the transit camp, where he became so ill that he was sent back to the hospital. This time he was admitted, but the doctors could not deal with his injury so they shipped him off to distant Winnipeg.

He seems to have received the best of treatment in Winnipeg—but it came too late. The damage to his eye had become irreversible.

He was returned to Eskimo Point, arriving there well after the conclusion of his trial, which had taken place on September 20. Mounik and Iootna, in the prisoners' dock, had defended themselves by claiming that they and Ohoto had broken into the Sherritt Gordon building only because they and their people were starving. This was not deemed sufficient justification. Both men were found guilty and sentenced to three months' imprisonment.

Indeed, the law has a long arm. A year later, between two bouts in hospital during which doctors vainly tried to save his injured eye, Ohoto finally came before a judge. He, too, was found guilty as charged, but the judge was lenient. Ohoto's sentence was the three months he had already spent in custody and in hospital.

By midsummer of 1957, the planners at the Department of Northern Affairs had reached the conclusion that Henik Lake might *not*, after all, have been the best place to send the Ihalmiut. It was therefore decided to exile them yet again—this time to the end of a long finger of rock called Term Point that juts out into Hudson Bay not far south of Rankin Inlet.

Because of bureaucratic delays this new transportation could not be carried out until 1958, so the Ihalmiut were fated to remain where they were for another winter.

On September 20, fourteen hundred pounds of supplies, consisting largely of flour, were flown to the camps. To make sure nothing went amiss this winter, Corporal Gallagher announced he would make an air patrol in December and a sled patrol a little later on.

The Ihalmiut began the winter of 1957–58 with the meat of six or seven caribou and fourteen hundred pounds of store food. This to keep life in forty-eight people. They had no meat after the end of October and were catching very few fish. In October a few of the men made the journey to Padlei and brought back some supplies. However, by mid-November their dogs were gone, having been eaten or having died of starvation. Manpower alone could not transport enough food to make the hundred-mile round trip to Padlei worth the energy expended.

As December fell upon the Ihalmiut they dispersed, attempting to scrape some sustenance from an almost-empty land.

The days grew shorter and the nights colder. January began dragging its frigid weight across buried lakes and hills.

The winter darkness became a winding cloth.

5 The Ordeals
of Kikik

On the morning of April 15, 1958, the Circuit Court of the Northwest Territories convened in the beer-parlour-cum-recreation-hall of a nickel mine on the shore of Rankin Inlet, 150 miles to the north of Eskimo Point. Judge Jack Sissons took his place behind a kitchen table, while on his right a row of jurors shifted their bottoms uncomfortably upon a wooden bench. Awkwardly aware of the demands of propriety, an audience consisting of whites and Inuit, all dressed in their finest, tried not to drown out the proceedings with the clack and clatter of folding chairs. Outside the doubly insulated building a husky scrabbled in a pile of garbage, while a pale sun beat down on a still-frozen world.

The prisoner sat at the judge's right hand. Although she smiled steadily at the assembled court, her eyes showed so little comprehension that she could almost have been mistaken for a wax mannequin. In fact, she was a woman plucked out of another time and brought to an alien place to answer charges laid against her by an alien race.

Those to whom she had to answer had gathered from across nearly half a continent. The judge and Crown attorney had flown from Yellowknife, seven hundred miles to the west. A learned medical witness and the defence counsel were from Winnipeg, eight hundred miles to the south. One of several Royal Canadian Mounted Policemen had been flown in from Pond Inlet, eight hundred miles to the north. And there were officials from Ottawa, fourteen hundred miles to the southeast. All these had come great distances, yet none had come a fraction of the distance travelled by the woman who stood before the court as the clerk read the indictment against her.

"You, Kikik, of Henik Lake, stand charged before his Lordship in that you, Kikik, Number E1-472, did murder Ootek. ... How say you to this charge?"

During the long night of February 7, 1958, a great wind roared across the tundra, stripping unresisting snow from rocky ridges and sending snow-devils dancing like dervishes across the frozen surface of North Henik Lake. Driven snow scoured the darkness like a sand blast and no living thing was to be seen.

Yet there was life beneath the wind. On the shore of a narrow bay crouched two snow houses. Within their dark confines people listened to the high-throated wail of the wind and tried to discern a tremor in it that might presage a lessening of its violence.

There were five people in the smaller of the two *iglus*, which was hardly more than a snow-block barricade roofed with a torn piece of canvas. One of these, the year-old boy Igyaka, lay rigidly inert. He could no longer hear the wind.

Beside him on the sleeping ledge of hard-packed snow lay his two sisters. Kalak, the elder, had been born deaf and dumb during a starvation winter ten years earlier. She and seven-year-old Kooyak lay in each other's arms under a single ragged deer skin. Their parents possessed nothing else with which to cover the children's bloated bellies and pipe-stem limbs. Most of the few caribou skins the family had possessed at the beginning of winter had been eaten, as had their outer garments. Caribou skin could be food of a sort as well as raiment, so those in extremity were faced with a hard choice: perish from hunger, or perish from the cold.

Contorted by the paralysis of polio that had afflicted her in 1949, Howmik crouched motionless over a handful of white ashes. There had been no fire for three days. The darkness seemed to thicken until Howmik could barely see her husband, Ootek, who lay against the snow wall on the sleeping ledge staring at nothing visible to Howmik.

Big and burly Halo, his wife, Kikik, and their five children lived in the second snow house a hundred yards distant. Hunger had also laid siege to them, but Halo's prowess as a provider had kept the dark presence at bay.

Whereas Ootek sometimes lived in worlds apart, communing with spirits, Halo was a man of the here-and-now, pre-eminently an able hunter and provider. Ootek, slightly built and with no great physical stamina, had never been more than a mediocre provider, not infrequently relying on Halo to help feed his family. Halo, on the other hand, counted upon Ootek to protect them all from the unseen and the unknown. Together, the two men formed the yin and the yang of a small universe.

Faith in this little world was what had held them at Henik Lake into early February, by which time most Ihalmiut families were giving up the attempt to survive in this alien country and were trying to reach Padlei Post. Owliktuk, that most sagacious of men, and Ohoto, who was now blind in one eye, had been among the first to flee. The others, excepting only Ootek's and Halo's families, followed suit.

By the time Onekwaw; his wife, Tabluk; and an orphaned boy named Angataiuak attempted to escape they had nothing left to wear except cast-off white man's garments given them at the time of their transportation from Ennadai. They might almost as well have gone naked into the white winter wind.

They had not got far when Angataiuak stumbled, fell, and could not rise again. So death took him, and two days later came for Onekwaw. Tabluk survived only because Henry Voisey's post servant happened upon her and brought her to safety.

Ootnuyuk, a widow with two children, fled Henik Lake in late December, for she had read the portents. Successful in reaching Padlei, she told Henry Voisey that a young man named Kaiyai was lying in a snow shelter halfway to the post. She explained that he had frozen his leg. Then it had thawed and frozen again, after which it swelled until it looked like a dead fish and stank like one.

Voisey radioed Eskimo Point, asking for the police plane to bring Kaiyai to hospital.

The short days and long nights slipped by and no plane came. Kaiyai's wife, Alekashaw, placed him on a hand-sled and with two infants on her back set out to haul her husband to Padlei Post. She pulled the sled for eight days before her husband died. She and her children eventually reached the post, but by then her own feet were frozen marble white.

By February 8, only Ootek's and Halo's families remained at North Henik. They knew by then that neither Ootek's spirit helpers nor Halo's skills could keep them alive much longer. The time had come to flee.

But it was past that time for Ootek and his family. Having eaten most of the skin clothing and robes with which they had begun the winter, they were now trapped inside a snow house that was becoming a tomb. As the sickly winter dawn of February 8 brought a febrile light into his *iglu*, Ootek spoke to his wife:

"Now I will go to the trading post. In a little while I will return with food for all of us."

Howmik looked into her husband's gaunt, great-eyed face but made no comment. Although she knew he stood almost no chance of reaching Padlei Post, she held her peace. The child Kooyak, bowels twisting in agony from the glut of caribou hairs and crushed bone splinters that filled them, could not do likewise. She screamed. Whereupon Ootek, usually the kindest and gentlest of men, struck his daughter across her shrunken lips.

"I *will bring food!*" he cried ... and walked into the bitter dawn.

Although flight was no longer open to Ootek's family, it was still a possibility for Halo and his. That morning Halo took his ice chisel and fish jigger and, breasting a rising east wind, went down upon the lake to laboriously chip through two feet of new-made ice that sealed his fishing hole. There had been fewer and fewer fish of late, but Halo thought if he could catch only a dozen or so of the little trout that remained in that part of the lake, they might suffice to feed him and his family for the trek to Padlei.

By midday Halo had caught two fish. He took these back to his snow house.

Meanwhile Ootek had set off northward towards a goal he knew he could not reach. The rising wind buffeted him. He fell on his knees before it, then turned back, stumbling to the snow house of his lifelong friend and companion. Crawling into Halo's *iglu*, he crouched on the dirty snow floor.

They sat together, these two who had been closer than brothers. Halo offered Ootek the tail of a fish and Ootek wolfed it down. Then Ootek asked for, and was given, the fish bones to take home to his family. Yet still he waited. He was a shaman, so perhaps he knew what was coming.

After a long time Halo spoke.

"There is nothing left here. So, when this wind weakens, I have to take my family and go somewhere else. There are too few fishes in this lake. If we stay, we will all sleep like your Igyaka sleeps."

With those words Halo severed the bonds between two who had been as one for so many years. He cut them ruthlessly for he had no other choice. He did not look at Ootek as he picked up his line and jigger and went out into the storm to take up his vigil at the fishing hole.

What was in effect a sentence of death had been pronounced upon Ootek. For a long time he sat silently watching Kikik, who was his own half-sister. Then he rose to his feet and smiled strangely at her.

"Now I must go on a journey, Kikik. But first I will take Halo's rifle and shoot some ptarmigan so my children can eat when I am gone."

With this he picked up Halo's .30-30 and left the snow house. His body was weak but his will was strong enough to carry him as far as he needed to go. Leaning into the wind, he shuffled towards his other self.

Unseen, unheard, shrouded by snow eddies, he did not pause until he was only a single pace behind the bowed figure of his friend. The wind striking through his scraps of torn parka warned him he must finish quickly. He raised the rifle and fired a bullet that shattered Halo's skull.

The wind swallowed the thunder of the shot. Ootek made his way laboriously back to Halo's snow house and stood the rifle in a drift at the doorway before crawling inside.

Ootek had become Nemesis—but he was a weak and tragic emissary of the fates. He could not even raise his arms until Kikik gave him a cup of hot water. The warmth revived him a little, but his unintelligible words—the kind of words a shaman speaks to spirits—disturbed his sister.

"You had better go home," she told him. Obediently he rose and left the *iglu*.

Outside the door he picked up the rifle and began brushing the snow off it. He was still standing in the storm's embrace when Kikik emerged. Apprehension had brought her out. The sight of Ootek cradling the rifle filled her with fear.

"Give me the rifle!" she demanded.

When Ootek made no reply, she stepped forward and grasped the barrel. The man would not let go. Brother and sister struggled for possession until Kikik lost her footing and half fell. She recovered to see Ootek bringing the weapon to his shoulder. His movements were so painfully slow that she had time to push the muzzle aside. He fired, but the bullet whined harmlessly away into the storm.

Desperately, Kikik threw herself upon him. Stronger, better fed, and impelled by fierce anxiety for her children, she overpowered him. Ootek fell and she upon him. Even her slight weight was enough to pin him to the snow. He struggled weakly as Kikik shouted to her eldest daughter, Ailouak, to fetch Halo from the jigging hole.

Ailouak emerged from the *iglu*, glanced in terror at the struggling pair, then ran towards the lake. She was not gone long. Sobbing wildly, she emerged from the enveloping ground drift crying, "My father cannot come. He is dead!"

What followed had the quality of nightmare. Sprawling astride the feebly struggling body of the brother who was also her husband's friend and killer, Kikik knew what must be done. She was well fitted to be Halo's wife, for she, too, was made of adamantine stuff. Her children would live! And of the several obstacles that lay between them and survival, Ootek was foremost.

Again she called to the now-terrified Ailouak.

"Daughter! Bring me a knife!"

Close followed by her brother Karlak, Ailouak crept out of the snow house. Both children brought knives.

"I took the largest knife from Ailouak and stabbed once near Ootek's right breast, but the knife was dull and would not go in. Then Ootek grabbed the knife and took it from me, but as we struggled it struck his forehead and blood began to flow. Karlak was standing near so I took the small knife he handed me and stabbed in the same place, near the right breast. This time the knife went in. I held it there until Ootek died. ...."

Kikik placed the two knives upright in the snow by Ootek's head, then crawled into the *iglu*. She found the children hunched on the sleeping ledge, staring at her from black, depthless eyes. Brusquely she ordered Ailouak to follow and together they hauled Halo's hand-sled down to the jigging hole. Together they rolled the freezing body of husband and father onto the sled and brought him home to lie close to his song-brother.[1] The two were together again, and forever.

The effort exhausted Kikik and Ailouak. Re-entering the snow house they lay panting on the sleeping ledge.

"We will sleep a while," Kikik told her children, and there was a quality in her voice as daunting as the north wind itself. "And in the morning we will go to Padlei."

In Ootek's snow house the crippled woman, Howmik, with her two living children and one dead child huddled close together. Kooyak whimpered in her agony and Howmik gave her water. There was nothing to eat. Even water could be procured only at heavy cost for there was no fire and Howmik had to melt handfuls of snow in a skin bag warmed by her own slim reserves of body heat.

Howmik slept little that night. Ootek's failure to return seemed to mean he had actually set out for Padlei, in which case, she knew, he must almost certainly be dead.

Kikik did not sleep at all. Before dawn on February 9 the wind fell light, the sky cleared, and the temperature plummeted many degrees below zero. Kikik roused her children and gave each a cup of water in which a few scraps of deerskin had been softened. Then she bade them prepare to travel.

They set about their small tasks readily enough for there was no gainsaying the inexorable resolution in their mother's face and voice. Within an hour the few possessions essential for the journey had been lashed to the hand-sled. Then Kikik removed the canvas roof of the *iglu* and tore it into halves. One half she placed over Ootek and Halo. From the other she made a bed upon the sled for Nesha and Annacatha, who were too young to be able to walk far through the heavy snow. In any case, they had no outer clothing to protect them from the frost.

[1] An Inuit relationship comparable to "soul mate"

It was at this juncture that Howmik emerged from her *iglu* and hobbled towards the others. Shivering uncontrollably in her tags and tatters, she stopped in front of Kikik. She did not need to be told what was afoot. The implications of the laden sled were clear enough. She also knew that nothing was to be gained by protesting. She contented herself with asking if Kikik knew where Ootek was.

Kikik was evasive. He might, she said, have gone towards Padlei, in which direction Halo had also gone to break trail for her and the children.

Howmik nodded. "Maybe they are both dead by now," she muttered, half to herself.

Imperturbably, Kikik continued her preparations for departure. She and Howmik had been close friends for years, and she had often helped the crippled woman with domestic tasks. But all that was past and gone. She could do nothing more for Howmik. Nor for Howmik's children.

Howmik understood. As unemotionally as if she were concluding a casual morning chat, she said, "Well, I am pretty chilly now. I will go home."

Shortly thereafter Kikik left the camp at North Henik Lake. The hauling straps bit into her shoulders as she dragged the sled upon which Nesha and Annacatha lay. Eighteen-month-old Nurrahaq rode tucked into the capacious *amaut* in the back of her mother's now almost hairless parka. Karlak and Ailouak trudged behind the sled.

The snow on the surface of the lake was hard packed by gales and for a time the going was good. Seldom pausing to rest, Kikik forced the pace to the limit of endurance. By late afternoon she and her children had travelled several miles. Then Kikik saw something that must have made her believe they had escaped the hounds of fate.

Far ahead bowed figures moved slowly across the ice. Drawing upon all her remaining strength, Kikik screamed so piercingly that the distant procession slowed and halted.

Yaha; his wife, Ateshu; their six-year-old son, Atkla; and a young man named Alektaiuwa turned towards her. They, too, were making for Padlei, but Ateshu's tuberculosis-ravaged lungs and Alektaiuwa's frozen feet had slowed them to what threatened to become a fatal crawl.

Now Kikik joined them and told her tale. Yaha learned that his own sister, Howmik, together with her children, lay starving and abandoned only a few miles distant. But the only food remaining to Yaha's group consisted of two or three pounds of putrescent deer guts dug from beneath the snow at an old kill. This was all they had to fuel their bodies until they could reach Padlei. Yaha dared not turn back now. He could do nothing for his sister.

A straggling line of plodding forms moved slowly into the frigid evening until finally Yaha signalled a halt. Then, with Kikik's help, he built a curved wall of snow blocks behind whose slim protection all of them huddled until dawn greyed the void around them.

Although daybreak brought a bitter wind out of the north, the fugitives had no choice but to face into it ... and walk.

Dragging the sled, Kikik could not keep up. Inexorably the others drew away from her. By the time darkness fell, she was unable even to reach the little travel *iglu* Yaha built. Through the whole of that roaring night, she crouched in drifting snow with her children burrowed beneath her body.

In the morning Kikik struggled out of the drift that had all but engulfed them. As the light strengthened, she saw Yaha's *iglu* in the distance. When she and the children reached it Yaha had this to say:

"You can go no farther. You must stay here in this *iglu*. I will take your sled to haul my wife. With its help we may go fast enough to reach Padlei before we die. Then help will be sent to you. Perhaps the airplane will come. If not, the trader will surely send his dog team. You and your children must stay here ... and wait."

There was nothing else for it.

Kikik watched impassively as Yaha and his family departed. Later she managed to gather enough twigs to light a fire and melt enough snow for each of the children to have a small drink. She was even able to squeeze a few drops of bluish fluid from her shrunken breasts for Nurrahaq. There was nothing for the other children. Six starving people huddled together under their scraps of canvas and waited—while the wind tolled.

Three days after leaving Kikik, Yaha and his family reached Padlei Post. Henry Voisey fed them and listened to their tale, then he radioed Eskimo Point, asking again for the police plane.

This time his plea was answered. On February 14 the RCMP Otter landed at Padlei, took Henry aboard as guide, then flew directly to the bay on North Henik Lake where Ootek and Halo had built their *iglus*.

Voisey and two policemen made their way to the now almost completely buried snow houses. One was empty. In the other they found Howmik and two children miraculously still alive, though reduced to skeletal caricatures of human beings. Light burdens all, the three survivors together with the body of little Igyaka were loaded aboard the plane. So also were the frozen corpses of Halo and Ootek.

Yaha had carefully described to Henry Voisey how to find the *iglu* in which he had left Kikik and her children. Nevertheless, the Otter flew back to Padlei without making any significant search for the missing family. Nor was any attempt made the following day. After overnighting at Padlei, the Otter flew out to Eskimo Point bearing the bodies of Halo, Ootek, and Igyaka. The next day it flew to Rankin Inlet to fetch a doctor back to Eskimo Point to conduct an inquest into the causes of death of the three bodies already at hand.

When Henry Voisey was later asked why, after the departure of the Otter, he had not immediately sent his post servant and dog team to bring in the missing people, his reply was that he had expected the police plane to return immediately from Eskimo Point.

No explanation has ever been offered for the plane's failure to return. Perhaps the decision makers concluded that Kikik and her children were already dead, so there was no urgency in finding them.

Huddled together in the frigid darkness of Yaha's travel *iglu*, Kikik heard the double passage of the plane. When that day drew to a close without help reaching them, she concluded none would come. Next morning while the Otter was winging its way to Rankin Inlet Kikik placed Annacatha and Nesha in a piece of canvas folded in such a way as to make a crude toboggan upon which she could haul them. Then the mother and children who had eaten virtually nothing for seven days, and little enough in the preceding weeks, set out once again for Padlei.

Theirs was an almost insensate action. Staggering like demented things they moved a yard or two, then paused as Karlak or Ailouak collapsed. Blackened by frost and as gaunt as a starving dog, Kikik would rest for a few moments then remorselessly, relentlessly, goad them to their feet.

She drove her children with an almost lunatic obsession. She drove herself even harder. During the six hours of daylight she moved her charges *two miles* closer to the goal that still lay almost thirty miles away.

When night fell, Kikik lacked the strength to build any sort of shelter. All she could manage was to scoop a shallow hole in a drift. In this depression the six then huddled, while the ice on nearby Ameto Lake cracked and boomed in the savage frost.

When the grey dawn began to lighten the east, Kikik faced the most terrible decision of her years.

She and her children could not *all* continue. She could not save them all.

Quietly she roused Karlak and Ailouak and forced them to their feet. Then she drew a flap of canvas across the pinched faces of the two little girls who lay sleeping in the makeshift sled. While the elder children watched, mercifully uncomprehending, she laid some sticks across the hole then piled snow on top of these.

Early on the morning of February 16 three figures moved like automata over the white face of a dead land. Behind them, two children slept.

Late on the morning of February 16 the police plane finally returned to Padlei, picked up Henry Voisey, and resumed the long-delayed search for Kikik and her children. The searchers flew directly to Yaha's travel *iglu*.

It had long been empty.

Airborne again, the Otter lumbered uneasily through the fringe of darkness while those aboard strained their eyes for movement on the snows below. Night was now rushing into the land. Turning back for Padlei, they passed low over the ruin of a long-abandoned trapper's cabin. Outside it stood a human figure, arms upraised in the immemorial gesture of a supplicant.

As Kikik watched the plane circle for a landing on the ice of a nearby pond, the indomitable being she had created out of her own flesh and blood began to crumble.

The plane came to a halt and soon two policemen were running towards her. They loomed over her, asking urgent questions.

"Where are your children?"

She was shaking so violently that Special Constable Gibbons had to grasp her around the waist and hold her up. She pointed towards the ruined cabin. Inside it lay three of her children.

"Where are the others?"

Slowly Kikik raised a skeletal hand and pointed westward into the gathering gloom. Gibbons bent close to catch the few words she muttered.

"She say they are asleep back there. She say she buried them."

The short day was ending. Insufficient time remained to investigate Kikik's story. There was barely time before dark to drop Voisey at Padlei, then fly on to Eskimo Point carrying Kikik and her surviving children to safety. However, young constable Jean-Louis Laliberte was left behind at Padlei with orders to take the post dog team and driver and recover the bodies of the missing children the following day.

Late in the brief afternoon of February 17 the dogs halted of their own accord near an unobtrusive hummock on the route to North Henik Lake. As the Inuit driver walked towards the little mound, he thought he heard a voice—a muffled, childlike voice. The sound froze him into immobility for he was one of those who still believed spirits inhabited the land.

Laliberte held no such belief. Tearing away snow blocks and a screen of branches, he uncovered two children. Annacatha was alive, if barely so. Nesha slept the long sleep.

And Kikik?

This woman who had mustered and maintained such transcendent fortitude for so long, who had brought life out of death, who had suffered what few human beings could imagine let alone endure ... she was imprisoned at Eskimo Point on the charges of having murdered Ootek and of having wilfully abandoned two of her children, resulting in the death of Nesha.

She remained a prisoner at Eskimo Point for almost two months. Her children were taken from her and, in what some observers saw as an act of deliberate psychic deprivation, she was not even told that Annacatha had survived until some considerable time after her arrest.

She had to endure several interrogations, for one of which she was flown to Baker Lake where the justice of the peace for the region ordered her committed to trial. She also had to submit to a searching examination by a Crown attorney flown in from Yellowknife. No defence lawyer was present on any of the occasions when, unable to speak or understand the language of her accusers, she was enmeshed in something of which she had no knowledge or experience—*kablunait* law.

She did not understand what was happening, only that she remained in jeopardy. She endured. She who had endured so much continued to endure.

In mid-April she was taken to Rankin Inlet to stand trial. There, at last, she found compassion when Judge Sissons virtually instructed the jury to bring in a verdict of acquittal.

The six men and women, most of them white, who held Kikik's life in their hands did acquit her on all charges, including "unlawfully causing the death of her daughter, Nesha."

Kikik's external ordeal ended at 9:00 p.m. on the evening of April 16. Under the glaring lights of the improvised courtroom, the judge glanced over his glasses at this woman whose face bore the fixed smile of one who does not comprehend what is happening. He spoke gently to her.

"You are not guilty, Kikik. *Not guilty* ... do you understand?"

Her expression did not change. She did not understand.

Then Douglas Wilkinson, a Northern Service Officer who had been appointed Prisoner's Friend, came forward and led Kikik into the unoccupied camp kitchen. He sat her down and gave her a mug of tea. After she had sipped it for a while, he spoke to her in her own tongue.

"Kikik, it is finished now ... all done."

Then at last the fixed smile faltered, and Kikik looked away from him towards the darkened window—and through it into a void beyond.

PART II

6 The Old ...

As soon as Norman Ross had finished his business at Eskimo Point we made ready to fly to the outpost of Padlei.

One of the last of the old-time trading posts, Padlei lay buried in splendid isolation deep in the interior to the northwest. In winter it could be reached by dog team from the coast in a week or ten days. A summer visit might involve two weeks by canoe. However, at any season a Beaver could (weather permitting) span the distance in a mere two hours.

Established in the 1920s to collect white fox pelts from the many Inuit then living along the shores of the Kazan River and the two great interior lakes called Angikuni and Yathkyed, Padlei Post was, by 1958, nearing the end of its commercial usefulness. Although white foxes were still abundant, only a handful of the People of the Deer who had once trapped them were still extant. Ross had told me this might be the last inspection trip to Padlei before the post was closed.

We had a fine day for the flight in. A few massive cumulus clouds floated in the high sky like a fleet of ceremonial barges. The vast green sponge of the coastal plain glittered and gleamed with sunlight reflecting from a multitude of ponds and lakes.

We had been airborne for an hour before rocky ridges began emerging from the muskeg below, like the heavily barnacled backs of antediluvian monsters. The land grew increasingly rough and rocky, riven by valleys some of which cradled groves of dwarf spruce and willow.

As we passed over a steeply humped island in the Maguse River, I spotted an upturned canoe. This, the first indication of a human presence we had so far seen, was, I would later learn, the grave of the last effective leader of the Padleiermiut (People of the Willows). A staunch pagan, he had been laid to rest under his canoe accompanied by his most valuable possessions with which to begin life anew on the Other Side.

We touched down on a lake-like expansion of the river running between looming ridges of saffron-coloured rock. Padlei Post stood before us: a neat, gable-ended cabin and a small storehouse resplendent in white walls and red roofs, forming a tiny oasis of civility in a shaggy wilderness.

Post manager Henry Voisey, with his wife, Charlotte, and their daughter, Mary, were at the shore waiting to receive us. Henry was a small, smooth-faced man in his mid-fifties, impeccably turned out in white shirt, blue tie, grey flannels, blue blazer, and polished brown brogues. Of mixed European and Inuit parentage, he had spent thirty years in the Company's service. Charlotte, considerably his junior, was a part-Inuit beauty from Repulse Bay. Incongruously, thirteen-year-old Mary was fair-haired. She wore a crisp, flowered frock of the sort considered stylish by girls her age in Winnipeg, where she spent nine months of every year at school.

Henry's greeting was as formal and deferential as if Ross and I were visiting dignitaries from Hudson's Bay House in London. The Voiseys then gravely escorted us up a swept gravel path to their little house, which had been polished to a fare-thee-well inside and out. Once we were settled in the snug living room, formality dissolved, to be replaced by the fabled northern conviviality of yesteryear. We were fed an enormous and elaborate dinner built around fresh lake trout, bottled caribou meat, roasted ptarmigan, and Newfoundland figgy-duff pudding for dessert. This was followed by peach brandy Henry had brought back with him from a recent trip to Winnipeg—a trip during which he had survived a liver operation and the removal of part of one lung.

Norman had warned me that Voisey had cancer but would not acknowledge it because to have done so would have meant an end to his tenure as master of Padlei Post. And Padlei was the only place Henry really cared about.

"'Tis my place," he told me. "The natives here are like my own folk. They knows me and I knows them. I don't say I couldn't do without them, but maybe they wouldn't do so well without me. That's the way of it, sir."

He did not know that the decision to close the post had already been made in far-off Winnipeg.

"It would kill him," Norman had said, "so I plan to keep Padlei going as long as I can. I hope for as long as he lives. I know you think the Company is just another piratical business outfit, Farley, but some of us *can* feel compassion. I'll be damned if I'm going to be the one to pull the plug on Henry Voisey."

Henry's domain was not overpopulated. Although in the past the Padlei region had harboured several Barren Lands trappers, none now remained. The Voiseys' only neighbours were a middle-aged Padleiermiut couple and their teenaged son—post servants employed to do rough work.

The remaining Padleiermiut, amounting to just seven families, were camped on the shores of Yathkyed Lake, fifty miles northwest of Padlei. They were the only other human inhabitants of a sixty-thousand-square-mile swath of Arctic prairie.

Members of his "gang," as Henry called them, were not encouraged to spend time around the post.

"Agin Company policy. I'm agin it too. Once you get natives hanging about they get lazy. Turn into post-loungers. Won't bring in fur. Will run up debt for whatever strikes their fancy. *If* you let 'em. For their own good, I don't let 'em. They're welcome here when they got fur to trade. Other times they oughta stay out on the land. If real hard times come, I'll do what I can to help out. Otherwise they're better off on their own. Natives is easy spoilt."

The help Henry could offer included makeshift medical assistance, limited quantities of "destitute relief supplies" (mainly flour, tea, and lard), and the services of his shortwave radio link to Eskimo Point.

That this assistance was by no means excessive is made apparent by Richard Harrington, photographer/writer, who visited the Padleiermiut by dog sled during February of 1950. The following quotations are from Harrington's illustrated book.[1]

"Henry Voisey came out to meet us [on arrival at Padlei] ... a trader of a bygone type, perfectly content at his lonely trading post. ... It was a calm household. Over supper Henry and I discussed fur prices, trapping, dogs, missionaries, and famine. White fox brought only $3.75 that year. Almost no market for them outside ... and there were few caribou.

"'Wherever you go around here,' said Henry, 'you'll see real hunger. Many of the dogs are dead. It'll take a few years to recover from this.

[1] *The Face of the Arctic*, Richard Harrington, Henry Schuman, New York, 1952.

You know how it goes: no dogs, no hunting ... it means no food, no new clothing. It means hungry people that catch any germ that comes along. You have sick people nailed to the spot and that means no hunting next year. ...'

"I asked what the missionaries were doing about the situation.

"'Praying, I guess,' said Henry."

Harrington visited several stricken Padleiermiut camps.

"On the lake called South Henik ... stood three skin tents and one igloo. In the igloo lived an ancient woman, resigned and ready to die. She and her man were destitute. Their dogs had died. The old woman sat in the dark igloo, sucking an empty, stone pipe. ... When I gave her some biscuits and tobacco I was surprised at her *Namakto*—thank you.

"Polio had struck this camp. One of the strongest of the young hunters had been a victim. He had been hauled by dog team to Padlei and flown to Churchill. From there, with other polio patients, he had taken off for Winnipeg. ... The plane crashed and all the passengers perished. His young wife, unknowing, was still awaiting him."[1]

Returning to Padlei Post, Harrington encountered "Bernard Fredlund, of the Northern Evangelical Mission, he lived in a nearby shack built with native labour. ... When I described the suffering I had seen, he said the people were doubtless being punished for their sins. When I told of a childbirth in a famine camp and described the difficult labour of the exhausted woman, he blushed, lowered his eyes, and edged away. ..."

Harrington was no firebrand but, as he says in his book, "My pictures would, I hoped, show the outside world what real suffering was. They would also show the strength, courage and ingenuity of an almost exhausted people. Maybe, after seeing them, the white men would stop referring to Eskimos as 'children' and 'incompetents.' ... They did not whimper and whine. ... They were unaware that a mass of

[1] Two Ihalmiut polio victims also died in this crash. They were among more than thirty deaths and forty cases of paralysis from the 1948–49 poliomyelitis epidemic that swept through the Keewatin Inuit.

government officials in Ottawa were looking after the welfare of the Eskimos. During this time of hunger the missionaries did not help; the RCMP had no instructions to help. ..."

In the event, the only help the Padleiermiut received came through Henry Voisey. He told me about it, albeit reluctantly.

"See, there wasn't much I could do. We'd run out of what they call destitute relief supplies. Only way to get more was by airplane. The police had a plane and could have flown stuff in. They never did it. Said they didn't have orders from Ottawa."

"So how did it end?" I asked.

"Six of my gang died," Henry responded shortly—and changed the subject.

Henry made no mention of a disaster that had ensued during the winter of 1950–51 when 22 Padleiermiut men, women, and children out of a population numbering 110 people died of famine and disease. It was not something he wished to talk about. Or, perhaps, since there was no future for Henry Voisey, there was also no past; there was only the here and now.

"There's forty-five natives on Yathkyed," he told Norman and me. "They'll come in at Christmas to trade their foxes. But they won't hang about and get foolish ideas. They'll go right on back to their camps. Sure, they get in trouble sometimes. Last year it was measles and four died. But so long as they stay out on the country, they'll be all right. If the missionaries don't get to them, that is."

Henry was no admirer of missionaries. One morning he took me three miles downstream from the post to the mission station established in 1950. It was a sprawling structure fifty feet long and twenty wide built of turf piled around a flimsy framework of spruce poles. The interior, hardly high enough to provide headroom, had been divided by pole partitions into rooms for the missionary, his wife, and the two children born to them during their five-year occupancy. The furniture had been laboriously handmade of local materials, including a huge double bed woven of spruce branches. The stove was an ingenious contrivance made from ten-gallon oil drums. It was designed to burn willow branches, twigs, and "logs," which, in Padlei, did not exceed two inches in diameter.

The cave-like interior of the largest room was dark, dank, and foul smelling.

"This was the church part," Henry explained. "Big enough to crowd in fifty or sixty natives. Trouble was, the natives never came.

"My gang's still pagans; always will be, I hope."

7 ... and the New

The day we were to depart for Rankin Inlet on the Hudson Bay coast to the northeast of Padlei dawned grey and threatening. Henry Voisey sniffed the air and announced:

"Goin' to be thick'a-fog out along the bay. You fellas oughta wait for better weather."

Al's response was to point to a flock of mergansers taking off from the river.

"Ducks are flying, Henry."

With which Al ambled off to get a forecast on the Beaver's radio.

"Churchill and Baker Lake are socked in," he reported. "Can't contact Rankin, but Chesterfield don't sound too bad. We could likely get in there if we had to. Let's give it a go."

As we lifted off into a lowering sky, GQW's cabin was damp and cold, but smelled wonderful. The usual odours of gasoline fumes, oily metal, and unwashed clothing were ameliorated by the savoury aroma from a pot of fish stew Charlotte Voisey had thrust upon us as we clambered aboard.

"In case you boys have to put down and spend the night in the country, this'll keep you warm." A thoughtful send-off.

For an hour we flew low over ridges reticulated by caribou trails etched into the living rock by the passage of countless hooves. But all were old. Of living deer, or recent sign thereof, we saw no trace.

The country had several curious aspects. One was a sequence of ancient gravel beaches ringing solitary hills almost to their crests, or snaking across the intervening countryside in parallel but sinuous lines. The effect was as if a primal titan had been experimenting with contour plowing. Although now high and dry, these beaches had been at sea level until the mighty glaciers melted away and the land, freed of their colossal weight, rebounded. I have combed such relict Arctic beaches in the interior a hundred feet above present sea level and found chalky, fragile seashells that had been washed ashore eight or ten thousand years ago.

Equally spectacular relics of the Ice Age were saffron-coloured, snake-like ridges wriggling over the country from horizon to horizon. Known to geographers as eskers, these meandering sand and gravel embankments are the "casts" of long-vanished rivers that once flowed under, and even through, the melting ice sheet. Eskers roam across the

Arctic for hundreds of miles with almost total disregard for existing topography and drainage systems. Their steep-sided embankments suggest the constructs of some long-vanished race of manic railroad builders. The level crests are used by caribou, wolves, and human travellers as convenient highways across difficult terrain.

At length Rankin Inlet opened before us, a thirty-mile incursion of Hudson Bay into a range of ancient mountains that time and glacial ice had ground down to massive mounds. It was a primordial scene unmarred by works of man—with one notable exception.

The head frame of a mine rose from a peninsula in the north-western corner of the inlet.

North Rankin Inlet Nickel Mine was a sprawling complex of raw and ugly buildings silver-powdered with dust from the crusher mill. There being no hospitable sand or gravel beaches along the nearby harbour, GQW had to splash down on a pond several miles inland from the mine. We were ferried back to the site in a decrepit jeep, to be received (not welcomed) by the mine manager.

Andy Easton was a huge, shock-headed, bellowing sort of a man who brooked no nonsense.

"This is mine property for ten miles in all directions. If you break any of our rules, off you go right quick! Such as: stay away from the Eskimo village unless you're asked there by an Eskimo. And when you meet an Eskimo, treat him like you would me or any other white man. I hope you can feed yourselves and find your own shelter. If not I suppose we'll have to put you up in the bunkhouse. In case you're tempted to stay too long, that'll be twenty-five bucks a day per head. Any questions? I'm busy now. Goodbye."

Easton's bark turned out to be worse than his bite. In the event, he gave me the run of his domain.

Prior to 1946 the peninsula upon which the settlement called Rankin Inlet stands had seldom been visited except by Inuit hunters. In that year a prospector came across an outcrop of nickel-bearing ore, but the find was judged to be too remote for profitable exploitation. It was not until the Cold War sent nickel prices rocketing that a promoter undertook to bring Rankin into production.

In 1955 diamond drilling revealed a pocket of very rich ore in the middle of a lode of only moderate value. It was clear from the outset that any "development" would essentially be a high-grading operation doomed to a brief if gaudy existence.[1]

Despite the lack of long-term prospects, the *idea* of a modern mine at Rankin fascinated bureaucrats and politicians in Ottawa who were then touting exploitation of the Arctic as the engine for an economic resurgence. Furthermore, the creation of such a mine seemed to offer a God-given solution to the problem of what to do about the Inuit, whose rapidly deteriorating condition was becoming a social and political embarrassment. The precedent that could be established by a mine at Rankin was seen as a forerunner of a New North.

Heavily subsidized by Ottawa, work at Rankin was begun. Briskly encouraged (and sometimes directly pressured by local authorities), Inuit from all over the eastern Arctic began arriving at Rankin, where, so they had been told, they would find work, schools, medical care, housing, and all the other benefits trumpeted by proponents of the white man's way of life.

By the time I arrived at Rankin in 1958, the mine had been in operation for two years and a so-called infrastructure had been established. Three hundred and forty Inuit were living at a place where, six years earlier, there had been none. But of that number, half the adult males had yet to find employment and only fourteen families had houses. The rest were sheltering in shacks and tents they had erected near the harbour.

Tents and even shacks can provide healthy living conditions in the north—providing (as was once the case) enough dogs are in attendance to dispose of organic garbage and human waste.

Unfortunately, dogs were forbidden in and around the "Eskimo village" at Rankin. In fact, the RCMP shot loose dogs on sight. Since no

[1] The mine ceased operations in 1962.

substitute sanitation system had been provided, the ground around and between the habitations was so thickly strewn with ordure and garbage that I could understand why Easton discouraged visitors.

There was no public health presence at Rankin. The only medical service was provided by a first-aid man at the mine's sick bay. Easton tried to ensure that anyone in dire need would be flown to Churchill in a company-owned, war-surplus Anson derisively known as the Bamboo Bomber, but this was only possible if, and when, the Anson was fit to fly.

Government participation in the planning and building of a properly serviced community had been minimal in all respects. Educational facilities consisted of a one-room schoolhouse provided by the mine though staffed by a teacher hired by Ottawa. The teacher was not a success. When Easton asked him to conduct classes in English for adult Inuit, he gathered thirty men and women together, seated them on the schoolhouse floor, and ran a toy truck back and forth in front of them while loudly repeating: "Truck ... truck ... truck. ..." Few students returned for a second lesson.

"He complained they wouldn't show up for classes," Easton remembered, "so I said what the hell did he bloody well expect? These people wanted to learn English, not play kids' games with a half-wit."

Easton's attitudes and methods antagonized many white residents of Rankin—especially the two Roman Catholic priests, an Anglican minister, and the ubiquitous evangelical missionary. They all complained that Easton was obstructing their attempts to bring the heathen to God.

Easton countered that the missionaries were "a bloody pain in the ass. They feud like a bunch of castrated hillbillies and don't do a damn thing to help with the real problems of the Eskimos. Which are physical—not spiritual. I wouldn't have let a damn one of them in here, but the company president is a good RC and he insisted the Oblate Order could come in. So I opened the door to the whole lot. Let them fight it out among theirselves."

The Inuit got on well with Easton. They seemed pleased to be able to "help him" work the mine. One Inuk miner told me, "Andy know what we need, and he look for that. In old times always one man in camp was the smartest, know more stuff, could help others pick what to do. He was camp boss. Andy camp boss here."

I asked this former seal hunter how he felt about going underground.

He grinned. "First time I so scared I nearly shit. But if Andy say okay, we don't worry. 'Be careful,' he say, so we be good and careful. Nothing bad happen down there. You come down, we show you."

At that time the Rankin mine was unique in Canada in that all its underground workings were in permafrost. The rock was permanently frozen to a depth of at least seven hundred feet (as deep as diamond drills had penetrated), and in consequence the temperature within the shafts and galleries remained a steady twenty-seven degrees Fahrenheit, winter and summer.

This was strange enough, but equally remarkable was the fact that most of the miners had, until only a few months previously, been living in tents and snow houses while hunting caribou and seals for a living.

When the mine first opened, its managers assumed that "Stone Age Eskimos" would be of no use except as brute labour—and perhaps not even for that. So professional miners were hired "outside" and flown to Rankin. Not surprisingly, many proved unable to cope with the climate, the isolation, and the permafrost conditions in the mine itself. Turnover was very high; productivity was low; and the company soon found itself experiencing serious financial problems. For a time it even appeared the mine might be forced to close. It was at this juncture that a new manager was hired.

Andy Easton arrived at Rankin early in the spring of 1957. He brought with him a reputation for making remote mines prosper under the most difficult conditions and for fostering amicable rela- tionships with native peoples. He concluded there was no need to go any farther afield than Rankin itself to find workers. Within days he was offering Inuit straight in off the land the opportunity to apprentice for any of a dozen different jobs.

He found no shortage of takers. By August 1957, the transient whites at the mine were largely gone and their jobs were being done by "Stone Age anachronisms." At the time of my visit the mine employed 120 people, of whom 84 were Inuit who were doing most of the actual mining. The remaining non-natives were mainly office workers or technicians. Although southerners owned the mine and took the profit, it was essentially an Inuit operation.

Donning armoured boots, safety hat, and a slicker, I went below to have a look. The cage man who took me down was an Inuk. He lowered me into the abyss with the calm of one who had been doing this all his life. Yet just two months earlier he had been living in a tent out on the Barrens, possessed of less knowledge about mines than I had about the interior of Mars.

Below ground, I found the ice-sheathed walls, the stench of high explosive, the shattering roar of compressed air locomotives and mucking machines distinctly unnerving. It seemed almost inconceivable to me that the human beings moving through the gloom around me could have so recently stepped into this cockpit of the machine age.

I watched as, small, nimble, and lithe, they expertly manoeuvred locomotives to the cage and sent cars of frozen rock to the distant surface. I watched them at the controls of thundering mucking machines, making the rattling giants obey their wishes as docilely as well-trained sled dogs. The simile seemed apt, for one of the mucking machine operators had driven his team five hundred miles south from Igloolik the previous winter to take this job.

Back at the surface I lunched in the crowded, noisy cook shack with Paul Proux, the mine captain. Paul was from Quebec. I asked him how he liked working with Eskimos.

"I tell you, my friend, the day every man below ground here is Esquimaux, that day I don't have no more worries. Those guys, they are good miners as ever I see. They don't have the accidents like white guys underground. They take big pride in what they do. They laugh a lot but watch close too. When I come here, I don't think we make miners out of Esquimaux. Now, I think they make better miner out of me."

I asked Easton if there was any truth in a recent newspaper interview given by one of the Oblate priests, accusing the mine of exploiting the natives as cheap labour. Easton snorted, and pointed to a wall chart showing monthly wages and bonuses paid. On average, Inuit working underground were earning *higher* wages than whites. One had earned the fantastic sum of $750 in the preceding month.

"There's no such thing as natives and whites around here," said Easton with some pugnacity. "There's only working men. Pay rates are the same for all. Good men get good pay."

I asked if the other white employees of the company felt as he did.

"They better! Or they're on the next plane out. But we don't get many guys like that. After a few weeks working, sleeping, and eating in the same bunkhouse with Eskimos, a lot of southern guys get to feeling a little bit inadequate. So they work harder, and act better. It all works out."

Of course, Easton's enthusiasm for Inuit employees had its practical side. "When you got good men living right on your doorstep that *want* to work for you, you'd be a goddamn fool to hire guys from two thousand miles away. Guys who hate the climate, get bored out of their minds in the north, would as soon make trouble as dig ore."

Easton's dream was to put the entire operation (except for top management and technicians) into Eskimo hands in just two years. He believed most of his Inuit employees could learn to read and write and even do office paperwork within that length of time. He already knew they could do almost everything else.

When I dared touch on the delicate topic of the mine's longevity, he replied without the defensive bluster I anticipated.

"Yeah. I know it doesn't look good right now. But exploration and drilling programs could prove up more prospects. Long-term prospects, not just get-rich-quick ones. Any good mining engineer will tell you this country's full of minerals just waiting to be dug.

"You know, mining could be like kind of a magic bridge between these people's old world and the new one they have to live in now. ... If governments and the industry *want* it to happen it'll happen. I believe that, Farley."

There was no doubt but that Andy Easton was doing his best to make the dream a reality. He had seriously antagonized the all-powerful Hudson's Bay Company by bringing a cash economy to people who had previously been enmeshed in the monopolistic debt-and-barter system of the fur trade. He had already brought the first non-religious school (such as it was) to the Arctic. He had guaranteed to fund a proper hospital as soon as the government agreed to provide a doctor. He had built fourteen small but comfortable wooden houses, equipped with electricity and running water, for the families of his Inuit workers, and he intended to build as many more as might be needed. Moreover, he was ruthless with whites who came into the community with the idea of taking advantage of Inuit naivety in business or other matters. As one of his white employees said, half-seriously, half-facetiously:

"Andy's a tough hombre, *if* you happen to be white. If you're a native, well, Jesus Christ, he might mother you to death."

What did the Inuit think about it all? I talked to a good many and found few detractors. Shiniktuk, a man of sixty who had acquired a pithy command of English while working for the RCMP, was typical.

"One time," said Shiniktuk, "lots of seals, plenty deer. Then white man come and pretty soon get too many killed. Then everybody get goddamn hungry. People die. Kids die. Maybe police give some dirty flour full of bugs. Maybe missions give some old clothes, got bugs in it too.

"Now we get work. Can buy good food, good clothes. Can send kids to school. No goddamn way we going starve no more now. No way white men all the time going to say do this, do that, just because they want. Now *we* talk."

Shiniktuk could talk all right. One of his jobs was to act as marine pilot for Rankin Inlet. Earlier that summer he had brought in a big British ore carrier. The captain, unnerved by the presence of a squat little Eskimo at the helm, fidgeted a lot and kept making suggestions. Finally Shiniktuk turned and politely asked, "You can pilot boat in here?"

Reluctantly the captain admitted he could not.

"Okay," said Shiniktuk, tightening his grip on the wheel, "then you goddamn shut goddamn mouth."

An early shot, perhaps, in what some Inuit already saw as a struggle to reassert their freedom to do, and be, what they chose to do and be.

During my time at Rankin I talked to as many people as I could find who had been involved with the Kikik affair. There weren't many. None of the Ihalmiut nor any of the officials who had taken part in the trial were available, though I did talk to some of the jurors.

The day before we were due to leave, Andy Easton made a suggestion.

"You want to know more about the Kikik business? You oughta talk to Doug Wilkinson, the NSO at Baker Lake. You'll be stopping there, so Ross tells me. Doug was here all through the trial and he speaks the lingo like a native. Most of the rest of the government guys up here are full of bullshit, but Wilkinson will level with you. I'll radio him you're coming, *and* that you're bringing along a little something from me. He'll know what I mean."

In 1958 everyone in the Arctic lived at an unconscionable distance from a liquor store. Andy was offering me an open sesame to Baker Lake. I was properly grateful, although neither he nor I had any idea how far afield his introduction would lead me.

8 Vatican of the North

Chesterfield, our next stop, lay sixty miles northeast of Rankin at the head of the great inlet of the same name. The day was fine and the flight short and uneventful. An elephantine hide of eroded rock below us offered little to attract my interest except for several snow-filled valleys.

Crouched on a rock-ribbed cape, Chesterfield was embedded in a matrix of ponds, tidal pools, and muskeg swamps. The place swarmed with mosquitoes in such numbers as to make the lives of red-blooded creatures a torment.

GQW swung over a scrabble of shacks and shanties loosely clustered around a group of monumental wooden structures that included a huge church and several gaunt, grey structures of Dickensian oppressiveness. These constituted an enclave familiarly known to non-Catholics as the Vatican of the north. It harboured the main central and eastern Arctic operations of the Oblates of Mary Immaculate, the Roman Catholic missionary order better known as the Oblate Order.

Some distance away gleamed the familiar white walls and red roofs of a Hudson's Bay Company compound. Al brought the plane down on the shallow harbour and taxied to the Company dock.

We were greeted by the post manager, bluff and amiable Bert Griffith, and his six-year-old son, Paul. While Al checked GQW's engine and Norm went off with Griffith to the Company store, Paul took me on a guided tour of the settlement.

Chesterfield was alive with birds. Snow buntings and longspurs intermingled with flocks of least sandpipers pursuing mosquitoes as avidly as the mosquitoes were pursuing Paul and me.

"That's where the black men and the grey ladies live," Paul told me innocently, pointing to the Bishop's Palace. Several black-clad priests of the establishment did indeed live there, but doubtless the Grey Nuns who served the hospital and the school lived elsewhere.

Next to the Palace stood a particularly austere-looking residential school that served much of the east-central Arctic. There was also a two-storey wooden hospital and a singularly grim-looking students' hostel. Although all of these except the Bishop's Palace had been built with funds from the federal government and were operated largely at government expense, they were nevertheless Roman Catholic institutions. Anglicans did not object to this arrangement since they enjoyed similar privileges in other settlements, especially in the western Arctic.

In late August, Eskimo children of grade-school age were flown to Chesterfield under RCMP escort from Baker Lake, Igloolik, Coral Harbour, Repulse Bay, Pelly Bay, and other far-flung settlements. Here they were destined to remain until June of the following year. As many as ninety were crowded into the hostel where they lived chiefly on beans, bread, and fish. In years to come I and the world at large would hear more about what this incarceration meant to Inuit children, but at the time of my 1958 visit the dark currents underlying the mission school system had not yet surfaced.

The settlement appeared oddly, even ominously, abandoned. We encountered nobody until we came upon a tent pitched near the outskirts. A young woman clad in jeans and a nylon jacket, and an aged crone in worn skin clothing, with faint tattoo marks on her cheeks, sat on the ground in front of it. They were chopping up arctic char with the curved women's knives known as *ulus*. They nodded at Paul. Later I would be told that the young woman had a "service connection" with the all-male staff of Chesterfield's Department of Transport radio station. Presumably the old lady was the duenna. These two were amongst the few adult Inuit then resident at Chesterfield, most of the rest having gone to Rankin in search of jobs.

Paul and I took brief refuge from the mosquitoes in the RCMP barracks. Paul had a message to deliver to Corporal O'Halloran, the NCO in charge. It was an invitation to join Ross, Al, and me for dinner at the Griffiths.'

The corporal, a broad-faced farmer's son from Prince Edward Island, was delighted to accept.

"Not too much social life up here," he explained. "Till I got posted north last summer I never figured I'd be spending my lifetime talking to husky dogs and Eskimos. Be a nice change to have a yarn with you guys. Besides which, Mrs. G. is a hell of a cook."

Mrs. Griffith, rosy and beaming, gave us a memorable meal consisting principally of steamed arctic char in a chopped-egg sauce, followed by deep apple pie drenched in rum and butter. Then, "full as pups," as Al put it, we retired to a snug living room for hot toddy and talk.

Mrs. Griffith tried to persuade her son to go to bed, but Paul would have none of it.

"I wanna hear the stories," he insisted, "specially about the corporal's crash."

"You've heard that enough times," his father remonstrated, "and it wasn't his crash anyhow."

"I wanna hear it again!"

"I'd like to hear it too," Norman interjected.

"Yeah," said Al. "I knew the pilot. But I never heard first-hand what happened. Sure would like to hear your side of it, Corp."

"The middle of last February," Corporal O'Halloran began, "I got a radio call to go to Rankin. Nothing serious, but I was due to patrol there anyway so the Eskimo [special constable] hitched up the detachment's dogs and off we went.[1] Was only a two- or three-day trip in good weather.

"Dr. Patrie, the doctor at the hospital here, had been on a course down south and he showed up at Rankin in TransAir's Norseman a day after I got there. Had a couple of patients with him in the plane: John Ayruia and his daughter Annie on their way home to Chesterfield after a session in Clearwater San for TB—a year for the girl and four years for John.

"Patrie'd told me often enough how he'd like to make a trip by dog team, so I said, 'Well, doc, now's your chance. I'm leaving for home tomorrow. Weather forecast's good and we might see a big old polar bear along the coast.' But the doc said he couldn't leave his patients. 'I'll fly on up in a day or two,' he said.

"Me and the Eskimo left next morning. The sky was clear, but it was thirty-five below zero and you can bet I didn't ride the sled much. I run along behind most of the day. It was a choice: run yourself to death or freeze to death.

---

[1] The special constable's name was Irkutlee. For reasons never given, O'Halloran referred to him throughout the story only as "the Eskimo."

"We holed up for the night in a cabin on the coast. The morning after was better. But the sky was kind of streaky, and pretty soon the wind got up again. By noon it was blowing twenty, thirty miles an hour and the ground drift was bad. Blue sky up above, but down on the sea ice, where we were, the drift was so thick you couldn't see the lead dog sometimes.

"I kept an ear open for the Norseman. The pilot, a guy called Wiggo Norwang—a Norskie, I think he was—had said he'd fly low along the coast and waggle his wings when he passed.

"About 3:30 we heard him go by. No mistaking the sound of a Norseman. But we never saw hide nor hair of the plane.

"It had started to snow and the ground drift was so bad it was getting hard to breathe. I figured we'd have to stop pretty soon and make some sort of a camp. Then about fifteen minutes after we'd heard the plane, we saw some black stuff showing up through the drift. At first I thought it was rocks. But we were out on the sea ice, or thought we were, a good way from shore.

"We stopped the sled and I asked the Eskimo, 'You know what that is over there?' He didn't know, but at the back of my mind I think I'd guessed. Then he says, 'Airplane!' and by then I could recognize bits and pieces scattered all around.

"The dogs had the scent and took off. The Eskimo upset the sled to stop them. I left him with the sled and ran for the plane. Didn't really want to, because I was afraid I'd find the people all smashed up and bleeding to death.

"Both wings were torn off; the engine was smashed off; the skis torn off. One side was torn out, and the top smashed in. First person I saw was John Ayruia. He was sitting in the snow near the tail. He had a broken collarbone and a broken arm, but when he saw me he was so scared I'd miss seeing the plane, he jumped up and ran at me waving his good arm and his broken one too.

"When I saw he was okay I worked along the side of the wreck and found the pilot sitting on the ice, bent right over. I pushed back his parka hood and he looked up. Wiggo has a habit of always shaking hands when he meets you, and the first thing he did was shake hands with me. His hands were bare—no gloves or mitts.

"'How did you know we were here?' he asked me. I explained we just bumped into them.

"'But who *told* you we were here?'

"He was pretty badly smashed up, with broken ribs, a smashed right leg, and a lot of bloody cuts.

"Dr. Patrie was thrown off to one side with both legs broken, eight ribs smashed, and a lot of teeth knocked out. The girl had a broken leg and some internal injuries, though we didn't know how bad any of them were until afterwards.

"When I found none of them seemed about to die, the question was: what could we do for them? First thing entered my mind was get them to Chesterfield. We didn't know how far that was, but it had to be maybe five hours away. They were too badly smashed up for that kind of trip, and we couldn't have taken them all anyway. They'd never have stood the wind and the cold, broken bones grating against each other over the rough sea ice.

"By then it must've been forty below and it was snowing hard as well as blowing. None of them was wearing country clothing—just what they needed for inside the heated cabin of a plane. They were still lying all around the wreckage, but I didn't want to move them till I had to, so I began wrapping them in caribou skins and our sleeping robes.

"The Eskimo was busy building a snow house. Now, good packed snow for an igloo isn't easy to find. But he found it and built a house big enough for all of them, though you couldn't stand up in it. It only took him about an hour and a half, which was good because much longer and some of them would have been frozen stiff, robes or no robes.

"Getting them into the snow house was a problem. We had no stretcher so we put them on the sled one at a time, cut a hole in the side of the snow house, pushed the sled inside, unloaded, and went back for the next one. After they were all in, the Eskimo sealed it up except for the door tunnel.

"Once inside I got our Primus stove going and made them coffee, then soup and beans from our grub box. I gave them some 222s, which was all I had for drugs. After that, all I could do was try to keep them warm and decide what to do next.

"Wiggo could talk and I asked him if he'd got an SOS through on radio before the crash. He said no, it happened too fast. I think his altimeter had froze up and he was flying blind in the snowstorm—a whiteout—and thought he was high enough, but wasn't. Flew right into the ice, and it's a miracle they weren't all killed right then. Maybe three miracles. The second was the plane didn't burn, which crashed Norsemen often do. The third was we found them so quick.

"Somebody had to head for Chesterfield. I sent the Eskimo, figuring by himself he might make it in three, four hours, which would mean that, with luck, the Department of Transport Bombardier snow machine could get to us before midnight.

"About 10:30 that evening it stopped snowing and the wind went down. By midnight it was nice and clear, but no sign of anybody coming. There wasn't enough kerosene to keep the stove going too long, but I didn't tell the people that. I hoped they'd doze off and sleep until help came.

"I don't think the girl knew what had happened. She was crying and yelling at first and I thought she was dying, but what she wanted was to be turned over on her back. When we picked her up to put her on the sled she said, 'Oh, my. The plane broke, eh?'

"The pilot and Patrie were frozen pretty bad and I tried to thaw out their feet and hands. Patrie wanted me to take his boots off, but I knew if I did I'd never get them back on because the feet would swell.

"Wiggo had it worst of all. When we loaded him onto the sled we hurt him a lot and he was screaming. That was hard to bear, but we had to go on doing it anyway. But he sure impressed me. In terrific pain, once in the igloo he never complained. It made me feel cheap when I rubbed his frozen hands trying to thaw them, and he'd just say, 'That sure feels nice.' His hands were frozen like a board. When he hit them together it sounded like hitting two pieces of wood.

99

"Patrie's and the pilot's feet were both froze, but at the time it didn't seem to worry them. They had been sure they were just going to die.

"John helped to keep the spirits up. When I made the coffee it was a little while before I got time to serve them, and John calls out, just like he was in a restaurant, 'Hey, coffee! Coffee over here!' By the time I gave him a cup it had got cool and he tasted it and said, 'Coffee not very warm, eh? But you crazy you think I'm going to die. I don't forget cold coffee!' He was real jovial.

"When they'd all had something to eat and swallowed the 222s, and I was trying to get them to go to sleep, John calls out, 'Where's the bean can?' 'Oh,' I said, 'you want more beans, John?' 'No, no, no!' he calls back. 'Want *piss* in can!' And he filled it three times.

"Was pretty uncomfortable in the igloo. I couldn't sit down and couldn't stand up. Once I went out to have a cigarette and stretch myself, and one of them fell asleep and upset the Primus stove. I got back before anything caught fire, but after that I didn't dare go out for more than a second.

"At Chesterfield the plane was way overdue. They knew something must have happened. Constable Massoti's wife asked him, 'If they've crashed, do you think there's any chance the boys'—me and the Eskimo —'will find them?' And Massoti answered, 'Not one in a million.'

"Soon after that the Eskimo showed up at the detachment. It had been a rough trip in and he and the dogs were pretty well played out, but he climbed right into the Bombardier to show them the way back.

"About 2 a.m. I fired off a flare I'd found in the plane, but there was no answer. I figured that was it for the night. I was just filling the Primus with the last of the kerosene when I heard the Bombardier. Gee, I was never so happy in all my life. Massoti's wife was in it and she was a trained nurse and just took over. She splinted them up and took the whole lot back to Chesterfield hospital. Next day an air force search-and-rescue plane picked them up and flew them to Winnipeg.

"When he was healed, John Ayruia got back as far as Churchill, and caught the measles there! Would you believe it, he's *still* in hospital in Churchill! Only his daughter's made it home so far.

"I don't know where Patrie is now. Down south for good, I'd guess. The pilot? Well, you know, he'd been just about ready to leave TransAir and start a little flying business of his own, but I don't think he will ever fly again."

While Ross busied himself with the post business, I prowled about the settlement—where I found myself something of a pariah. Word had reached the Oblates that the author of *People of the Deer* was in their midst and they reacted as if the anti-Christ had arrived. I found church, hostel, and school locked up tight. When I tapped on the imposing door of the bishop's mansion, I could elicit no response. I *did* see a pair of nuns peering at me from a hospital window, but when I caught their glance they hurriedly disappeared.

I wandered to the outskirts to visit the neat block of white buildings constituting the DOT radio and meteorological station. The four-man staff greeted me warmly, even to the extent of producing rum and coffee, then filled my ears with complaints about the hardships they were enduring.

"It's like being posted to the North Pole," the meteorologist said. "Sure, we get good grub and isolation pay and all that, but holy Jesus Christ it's lonely. The other whites up here treat us like trespassers in their private little world. The natives are okay, if you can stand the stink, but how in hell do you talk to them? And ten months of the year it's so goddamn cold if you step outside you freeze your knockers off!"

Another man, a veteran of the war, told me: "I see it more like some kind of concentration camp. It's run like one. The priests tell the Eskies what they can think, or can't. The Bay guys tell them what to do and when to do it. And the Mounties act like Gestapo, sticking their noses into everybody's lives and telling them to watch out, or else."

I asked what they thought of Corporal O'Halloran and found he was no hero in their eyes.

"The natives hate that guy. The Mounties have laid it down that all dogs in the north got to be tied up all the time. If not, they're shot. Mounties have gone into places like Eskimo Point and Rankin and shot fifty, seventy-five dogs at a time. Last time he did that at Rankin, O'Halloran just left the bodies lying about, along with a good many wounded that the locals had to finish off. Before his last dog-shooting spree, he came in here and ordered us not to let Rankin know he was coming, 'otherwise the Eskimos will have their dogs tied up before I get there.'"

It was too nice a day to spend in this kind of atmosphere so I went into the country.

I made my way slowly along a forbidding brow of shore rocks towards a distant point thrusting far out into Hudson Bay. Several miles from the settlement I came upon eight dogs chained to stakes, exiled to endure an insect-tormented summer until someone needed their services again. Fed once or twice a week, *if* they were lucky, they were hardly more than skeletons clothed in matted fur. Only their yellow eyes seemed alive. They watched my approach with fixed intensity until they understood I was not bringing food, whereupon they tucked noses under tails to partially thwart the clouds of mosquitoes and resumed their endless wait.

I passed several former Inuit camp sites, some of considerable antiquity, some recent enough to be littered with tins, bottles, and other rubbish. The rocks behind the latter were splashed with ruddy slabs of drying walrus meat from which shattered bones protruded. Presumably this meat, together with some putrescent seal skins with blubber still attached, was dog food.

At one point I clambered up the shore ridge and found the skeletal remains of three ancient whale boats—long, piratical-looking double-enders whose oak planks had split and silvered with time. They had been hauled into niches in the shore rocks well above storm-tide reach and had never been reclaimed. Rusted, smooth-bore guns and several harpoons lay on their splintered bottom strakes. I concluded they had been cached by nineteenth-century American whalers who, having effectively exterminated the large whales in Hudson Bay, never returned for these boats and gear.

The farther I walked along the great sweep of the point, the older the traces of man became. Stone tent rings gave way to collapsed mounds from which chalk-white whale ribs and lower jawbones protruded, proclaiming these places to have been habitations of the Thule-culture people who were the ancestors of the Inuit.

The point itself was a lovely place, wind-clean and sweetened by minute but potently perfumed tundra flowers. It was fringed by richly lichened rocks and yellow sand, and by a reef of marbled bedrock slashed by broad bands of garnet.

Great flaming clouds were now streaming across the Barren Lands far to the west, looking very threatening indeed. I turned my back and continued out to the tip of the point towards three stone *inuksuak* that so resembled human figures I almost hailed them before realizing my mistake. The only sounds came from a scold of arctic terns that skittered close to my head while a bevy of eider ducks lumbered up and away from one of the tidal pools.

At the sea-and-ice-eroded tip I found a comfortable boulder to rest my back against. Here I was joined by a starkly white Iceland gull, a species that had no business to be in this part of the world. But *I* had no business there either. Peering down at me, the gull hovered a few yards above my boulder before sliding away towards the great orb of the lowering sun.

Making my way back along the spine of the point, I came upon a frost-shivered ridge of bedrock, some of whose crevices had been capped with boulders to form stone crypts. Peering into one of these I saw a human cranium.

A glitter in the moss beside this ancient burial caught my eye and I reached down to pick up a half-moon-shaped piece of polished slate. It was an *ulu*, doubtless part of the grave goods accompanying whoever lay in the crypt. Foxes or ground squirrels had tumbled the *ulu* through the interstices in the rock for me to find.

The long day was drawing down. From the beach between me and the distant settlement, tethered and hungry huskies began to howl their miseries. They were answered, derisively, it seemed to me, by the high-pitched yelping of an arctic fox free to come and go as it pleased ... even as the unknown woman whose remains lay in the rock vault beside me had once been free to come and go at her own pleasure.

I thought sadly of the sled dogs and grimly of the children who would soon be crowded into the grey barracks in Chesterfield. Then I looked at the shining *ulu* in my hand ... and slid it back inside the crypt to lie again beside one who had never lost her freedom.

9 Baker Lake

Our next stop was Baker Lake, at the head of the great waterway including Chesterfield Inlet that thrusts westward into the heart of the Barrens for two hundred miles from Hudson Bay.

We had intended to make an early start but Al decided to change some spark plugs first. "Just to be on the safe side," so he said. But I suspect he deliberately delayed our departure because he knew what Mrs. Griffith was serving for lunch: fillets of sea trout with home-made mayonnaise, roast caribou hearts, and cloudberry (bakeapple) tarts smothered in canned cream.

We lifted off from Chesterfield in superb weather. I may have dozed for I do not remember much about the country except that the glaciers seemed to have swept it clean of almost everything except rock and water. I do remember the high inland plateau to the west flaming in the light of the sinking sun until its myriad lakes glittered like the shards of God's own shattered mirror.

We saw no sign that human beings had ever trespassed in this colossal wilderness, which made Al, most pragmatic of men, a little uneasy.

"That's some awesome lonely country, boys. I'd hate like hell to be trying to find a wife down there."

We were all relieved when an encrustation of tiny buildings revealed itself on the shore of Baker Lake's northwestern bay. We landed near a small freighter, the *Federal Trader*, which was anchored in the bay, and taxied to the beach.

Three men awaited us. One was Sandy Lunan, grandfatherly manager of the HBC post, on hand to greet his boss. The second was RCMP Corporal Donald Wilson, who shook hands with Ross, nodded at Al, and acknowledged my presence only by asking, suspiciously I thought, how long I planned to stay. The third was a tall, powerfully built, soft-spoken man in his late thirties who introduced himself as Doug Wilkinson.

"I'm the Northern Service Officer here. Would you be Hardly Knowit? ... if you'll pardon me using the tag some of the old Arctic hands have pinned on you. Yes, I got Easton's message. I can't speak for my department, of course, but I'll help you any way I can personally. My wife and daughter have gone south so you can batch in with me if you've nowhere else to stay."

Lunan had space for only two guests so I was glad to accept Wilkinson's invitation. He led the way up a stony slope to a recently erected, prefabricated log cottage that would have done credit to any prosperous southern summer resort.

My surprise must have been evident. Wilkinson chuckled:

"Nothing but the best for Northern Affairs. See, we're the new boys so Ottawa feels we have to impress the Mounties, the Bay, and the missionaries. The Old Guard don't take kindly to newcomers, which is too bad because, like it or not, we are the shape of things to come."

"You think that's going to be a better and happier shape?" I could not forbear asking.

"Ask me ten years from now. Meantime, come in and have a drink."

Wilkinson was one of a new breed of Arctic hands. Like me, he had served in the army during the war and had gone north afterwards, having had a bellyful of the lethal antics of civilized man.

He became a movie maker. In 1947 a film project took him to Eskimo Point, where he encountered his first Inuk. That meeting sparked a fascination with, and admiration for, the Inuit that changed his life.

During the next four years, Wilkinson and his wife, Vivian, travelled widely in the eastern Arctic filming the Inuit. As he became more and more involved with these people, so he became more and more concerned about their future. In 1952 he went north determined to live a full year *as* an Inuk in order to better understand them and their ways.[1]

He spent that year in the camp of a Pond Inlet man named Idlouk and engaged himself so thoroughly with the little community that Idlouk ended by adopting him. Towards the end of that year Idlouk wrote this testimonial, originally in syllabics:[2]

"I write that Kingmik [Wilkinson's Inuit name] is doing things exactly as the Inuit do. He is a good man. He will understand very well about us when he is through. He lives right with us. He does not tell false things about the way Inuit live and do things. Some of the

[1] His account of that year was published in 1954. Doug Wilkinson, *Land of the Long Day* (Toronto: Clark, Irwin and Co., 1954).

[2] Syllabics is a form of writing devised for the Cree but adapted to Inuktitut, the language of the Inuit.

other white men do not remain a long while with Inuit—but not Kingmik—he is a real Inuk."

High praise indeed.

Wilkinson's Arctic experience and especially his two National Film Board documentaries, *Land of the Long Day* and *Angotee*, brought him to the attention of Ottawa bureaucrats who were then proclaiming a new deal for the Inuit in conjunction with their vision for a New North. He was invited to join the Department of Northern Affairs in the newly created role of Northern Service Officer, and to bear a hand helping the Inuit through what was clearly going to be a most difficult transition period.

"I didn't necessarily believe their spiel. But there was no doubt a revolution was coming to the north and I figured I might have more influence if I was an active part of it. So in the fall of 1953 I signed up."

His first posting was to Apex Hill near Frobisher Bay (now Iqaluit), the de facto capital of the eastern Arctic. Here he found himself enmeshed in administrative detail and bureaucratic strictures, which was not the job he had in mind. In the spring of 1956 he asked to be allowed to work with the Ihalmiut who, he had heard, were to be moved from Ennadai to Henik Lake.

"In my opinion, a lot more information was needed before any move was decided on. I thought someone should be sent in to live with the Ihalmiut for a few months to properly get to know them and their problems, and only then make recommendations for their future, paying attention to what they themselves wanted. I hoped to make them my major project; but that idea got shelved on the grounds that I'd be more useful at Baker Lake, which was too far away from the Ennadai people. So the job of looking after them went to Bill Kerr, the NSO at Churchill."

Wilkinson did not arrive at his new posting until December 1956, when he and his wife and young daughter flew in to Baker to find an unfinished house, no furniture, no fuel, and (almost worst of all) no canoe, dog sled, or other trail equipment with which to travel the country and visit his new charges.

These consisted of four groups of Caribou Eskimos: the Harvak-tormiut of the Lower Kazan River; the Akilingmiut of the Lower Thelon; the Haningaiormiut of Back River; and the Quanermiut of Baker Lake itself. Numbering fewer than a thousand people, they were dispersed in camps of from one to several families scattered across nearly seventy thousand square miles of tundra. If the new Northern Service Officer was to be of any help to them it was imperative that he have the use of a dog team.

The Baker Lake RCMP detachment possessed a splendid team, though the police had a reputation for seldom making sled patrols. However, they would not lend their team to the Northern Service Officer. Eventually, as we shall see, Wilkinson found a partial solution to his problem by purchasing, and learning to fly, his own little airplane. But during his first, and vital, winter at Baker Lake he was largely confined to the settlement and its immediate environs.

He and I soon established a first-name relationship, but we had little time to talk during our first evening. We had barely finished a spartan supper of canned stew when a peremptory knock summoned my host to the door. He opened it to a narrow-faced little man wearing the look of doom and clutching some rustling papers in his hand.

Wilkinson introduced the newcomer in perfunctory fashion.

"Ernie Caygill, RN. In charge of the nursing station."

Caygill gave me a nod then announced a major emergency. He had, he informed us in sepulchral tones, identified the virus of contagious hepatitis in the urine of an Inuit patient.

"You realize just how serious this is, Wilkinson? Hepatitis has an incubation period of sixty days, which means it could have *already* spread right through the district!

"I'm quarantining the settlement. I've radioed for doctors and gamma globulin. I'm organizing the police and the missionaries to get out to the camps they can reach by canoe and bring in urine samples from everyone. I want you to fly your plane out to the distant camps. Tell the people to get in here, or at least send urine samples."

He paused and stared at each of us accusingly, as if we were somehow to blame for what was happening.

"There's no time to waste ... or there'll be a bloody epidemic on our hands!"

Abruptly he turned on his heel and left. Doug grinned ruefully at me as he shut the door.

"Bit of a character, Ernie. I'm nominally in charge here, you know, but he doesn't acknowledge that. Anyhow, I'm off to the radio station to let Ottawa know what's happening. Make yourself at home."

When he returned he showed me a copy of the message he had sent to his superiors in the Department of Northern Affairs. It began:

HAVE TO REPORT CASE CONTAGIOUS HEPATITIS STOP ALSO FARLEY MOWAT ...

"Don't know which'll shake them up the most," was his wry comment before returning to the subject of Caygill.

"Ernie's a sharp little bird, but he doesn't seem to realize I can't just drop in on the outcamps. Until I get a set of big-wheels—oversize, low-pressure tires—on my plane there's not many places I can set down on the Barrens.

"What I *can* do is spot the location of the camps so a float plane can find them and land somewhere close enough to check them out. Tomorrow, weather permitting, I'll go looking. Come along if you'd like. Though I warn you, I'm still pretty new to the flying game."

The next day dawned fine and clear. Doug's assistant, a young Inuk named Atungalik, ferried us by canoe across the bay to a landing strip under the brooding shadow of North Mountain.

Wilkinson's two-seater Piper Cub seemed incredibly frail and insignificant in this gargantuan landscape. Nevertheless, its engine started bravely and, after a bumpy take-off, we were away. Doug occupied the front seat. Crowded in behind him I felt somewhat as if I were riding on a bicycle built for two. There was no intercom. We communicated by horrendous shouting.

He had warned me that the camps we sought were widely dispersed. This turned out to be something of an understatement. We droned westward above the majestic, rapids-riven Thelon River for an hour without seeing a sign of human life, past or present. Finally, as we approached Schultz Lake, Doug spotted a single tent almost invisible amidst a sea of glacial boulders. Clearly the home of successful hunters, it was surrounded by caribou meat sliced thin and spread to dry over stones and bushes. The half-dozen occupants of the tent came tumbling out, waving a vigorous invitation to come down and pay a visit.

We could only wave back before climbing away to resume our search.

We flew north and west for the next two hours, and in all that vast immensity found only three more tents. Sugar lumps scattered across a football field could hardly have been more inconspicuous.

The Cub banked gently until she was on a homeward course. It was late afternoon before we landed under North Mountain to find a grinning Atungalik waiting for us beside a campfire over which he was broiling arctic char he had caught while we had been gallivanting around the country.

"You like plane better or dog?" Atungalik asked me as we ate char and bannock washed down with well-boiled tea.

"Well, a plane is faster. But with dogs you can stop and visit when you want."

He beamed with pleasure. "*Eeema!* Yes, yes! And if get lost, can eat dog."

That evening Doug talked about the empty land.

"It's astonishing. A region as big as our maritime provinces and New England combined. A productive region, with caribou and even musk ox. Lakes and rivers teeming with fish. Wildfowl by the millions. And yet, except for the people we saw today and a handful of others, there's nobody left in the whole country from Baker west to Great Slave Lake!"

"Aren't there still Eskimos at Garry Lake and along the rest of the Back River?" I asked.

"Not any more," Doug replied grimly. "Not after this spring. I guess you haven't heard too much about that. Not many outsiders have."

"Tell me then."

He got up from the table, carried our glasses to the sink, and, with his back to me, replied:

"Maybe some other time. Let's hit the sack. I've got a long day coming up."

Norman Ross had planned to spend some time here, but he now found it necessary to fly on to Bathurst after only a day. Because I hoped to learn more about the Kikik affair from Wilkinson, and because of mounting curiosity about what had happened at Back River the previous winter, I decided to remain at Baker. Regretfully I said my goodbyes to Norm and Al and watched GQW lumber off into the western wilderness.

After her departure, I set out to explore the community. Like most such Arctic settlements, Baker had begun life as a trading post. An immaculately maintained Hudson's Bay Company store, a warehouse, and Sandy Lunan's snug home still held pride of place on the east shore of the settlement bay. A weathered little Anglican church crowded companionably close to an equally worn bungalow, the home of the Reverend W. J. "Jimmy" James, an elderly Anglican priest who had recently been made a canon in recognition of thirty years of service here.

The Bay and the Anglican mission between them constituted what was left of the old Baker Lake. A scrabble of new buildings was now threatening to obscure the past. Brightly painted, but already scruffy-looking, prefabs housed a welfare officer, school teachers, a nursing station, a radio station, and sundry other government functionaries. A large school was under construction close to a partly finished Roman Catholic mission. Several plywood, steel, and aluminum buildings stood along dusty gravel streets cluttered with bulldozers, dump trucks, and piles of construction materials. These mostly housed scientists and technicians involved in investigations celebrating the International Geophysical Year.

While I was taking a cautious look at this modern development I was accosted by Canon James, who insisted I accompany him "back to the manse for a cup of tea and a chat."

Fearfully thin, stoop-shouldered, lantern-jawed, with eyes so preter-
naturally faded as to be virtually colourless, he could have been a cari-
cature of an English rural dean—except for his clothes. These
consisted of a bizarre mix of rusty-black clerical trousers, a flaming
plaid work shirt, and knee-length lumberjack's boots.

Jimmy James was clearly a character. To many Baker Lake residents
he was more than that. According to one of them:

"Poor old Jimmy's going dotty. No harm in him, but they ought to
send him home before they have to *take* him there."

He was the settlement's own Ancient Mariner. Seated in his dark,
dingy, musty little parlour, I listened while he whelmed me with frag-
mentary references to unknown people in unidentifiable places.

A gentle soul and an irredeemable romantic, he was not really part
of the world in which he found himself. For him it was a place of exile
inhabited by mostly alien creatures whom he viewed in kindly but
distant fashion. It had not been any dedication of his that had brought
him amongst them to serve their religious needs. It had been, as he told
me with surprising and embarrassing frankness, the unrequited love of
a woman—not love of God—that had sent him from his English home
to become a missionary.

As a young priest in the mid-1920s he had fallen deeply in love with
the wife of a fellow priest. This so overburdened him with guilt that he
felt compelled to volunteer for service in what was known in his circles
as Canada's Frozen North.

Sent to Baker Lake only a few weeks after reaching Canada, he
found himself cut off from everything he had previously known,
surrounded by heathen (and smelly) savages, with Sandy Lunan as his
only compatriot.

He survived by creating his own world, within which he lived the
imagined life he might have had in England. This had sufficed until a
few years before I met him. Then he had heard that the woman he
loved was now a widow.

"He started going to pieces," Sandy Lunan told me. "One day the puir
laddie would be all for flying right the way home to claim his bride.

Next day he'd be sure she'd want no part of the likes of him, so he'd crawl into his hole. He'd take no sup of food or water 'til I'd send my housekeeper over wi' a bowl of soup and a wee dram, and she'd stand over him 'til he downed it. I've told his bishop and I'd no' be surprised if they send him home before the year's out. Will the lassie have him or no? Weal, one way or t'other Jimmy'll be out of his pain."

Sandy Lunan was the chronicler of Baker Lake. At sixty-something (he would not tell me his age), he was a founding father of the place. Arriving in 1929 as a young clerk with the French trading firm of Revillon Frères, he had remained, after Revillon was bought out by the HBC, to eventually become the uncrowned King of Baker Lake. However, in recent years the Old North had suffered such changes that Sandy no longer felt at home in it. When I met him he was about to retire—for the third time in as many years.

A strict but kindly paternalist as far as the Inuit were concerned, Sandy was an inveterate gossip and a bottomless repository of Arctic lore.

He seldom visited the other whites, preferring his own well-appointed, if old-fashioned, house. This he shared with Akomalik, a jolly, gap-toothed woman of about his own age whom he carefully referred to as his "housekeeper," and with a sweet-faced apprentice clerk recently arrived from Aberdeen.

Sandy extended a convivial reception to visitors of all kinds, including me. The chief of a highland clan could hardly have been more hospitable, though Sandy did have his cutting edge.

"Trouble with you writers is you're easy taken in by the natives. They know how to play on a white man's sympathy, ye ken. Give 'em an inch and they'll take the bluidy mile. You have to be boss, and no mistake. Treat 'em like wee bairns and keep 'em in their places. Weal, laddie, I've done the best I could for 'em. No regrets about that. Now yon new chaps from down south is turning it all upside down. ... Time I was away out of it."

Sandy had a wealth of memories. One I particularly liked concerned a visit Anne and Charles Lindbergh paid to Baker in the late 1920s while seeking new worlds to conquer.

"They come down on the bay in their flying boat and my house-keeper and me met them at the shore. They talked pidgin English at us 'til I turned my Glasgie tongue loose. They come ashore wi' a basket of stale sandwiches and rotten peaches. Turned out 'twas all the grub they had aboard. When Akomalik served 'em up fresh baked bread, roast caribou, and mince pie, they tucked in like they'd no' eaten for a week.

"All well and good. Away they went. Years later somebody gie me a book they'd written about their trip. It told how they come down at Baker and found a Hudson Bay Company factor starving to death, and they saved his life by giving him their grub! *Their grub*! A dozen silly wee sandwiches, and peaches even the natives wouldn't touch. So you see, Mr. Mowat, how it is that some of us is a wee bit distrustful of writing folk."

The Lindberghs may have been the first aerial tourists to reach Baker Lake. They would not be the last. The summer of 1958 had already seen the arrival of four parties of wealthy Americans in privately owned amphibious aircraft.

"They dinna come to view the folk or the country," Sandy noted. "Only tae fish. Trophy fishermen, ye ken, looking for the grandest lake trout or char in a' the world. A few years back one crowd loaded their plane so heavy wi' char it crashed. Some Back River natives come upon 'em and carried word out, and the military flew in and rescued 'em."

Sandy paused to gaze speculatively out of his lace-curtained front window. "That was maybe too bad ... might hae taught they sports a lesson. The Barrens is nae a playground for the idle rich."

"What about the Back River people?" I asked. "I hear they were hit pretty hard last winter."

He shook his head. "I'll no' be talking aboot that. Best ask Mister Wilkinson. Or the Mounties. Or the priests. You *might* get to the truth of it ... if you was verra lucky."

Sandy had little use for Roman Catholic missionaries, or for most agencies of government. He was especially harsh in his criticism of the medical services.

"They doctors comes in maybe once a year by plane or ship and X-ray all the natives they can lay hands on. If the puir folk have the TB, and many do, they're shipped right out the day, to sanitariums away down south. They can be awa' for years and no word between them and those left behind. They might come back someday or they might die down south. Ye ken, they're a' verra fearful of being sent away, not knowing what'll happen to theyselves, or their families left behind.

"Breakin' up families can be the death of people here. Few women can keep going on their own, even with the help of relatives. And a man sent away is like to lose his dogs, his gear, and all the stuff he needs to feed a family when he comes back. *If* he comes back. When a wife and mother is sent out 'tis much the same thing. A man can't keep a family going in this country without a woman. But women is scarce, so often enough he has to give away his bairns. Some of the bairns with TB as get sent south can't even speak their own lingo when they come back. They're nae good tae their ane selves or anyone else."

One morning Doug rousted me out early.

"The hepatitis flap's getting worse. Some Eskimo men came in last night from Prince River so sick they could hardly handle their boat. I'm off to their camp with the Mounties to fetch in the rest of their families. Want to come along?"

We made the journey in two sea-going canoes driven by outboard motors: Doug and I in one, and two RCMP officers in the other. It was a rough, cold trip under lowering skies, pounding into the teeth of a stiff easterly that was pushing up four-foot swells. High-powered outboards may have their virtues, but they take their toll. The drubbing endured by the bow passenger (me) threatened to permanently damage my kidneys.

The Inuit camp at Prince River, twenty miles east of the settlement, stood beside a sandy estuary. It was an attractive setting: a small cove guarded by south-facing hills sheltering a three-foot-high copse of willow scrub. The camp itself was less attractive, consisting of a pair of tents set in a litter of fish guts, human and dog excrement, broken glass, rusted tins, and nameless debris.

My repugnance must have been apparent to Doug.

"You won't see much worse than this, Farley. These are some of what's left of the Back River people. They were in bad shape when the RCAF flew them south three months ago. They were too far gone to go out on the land hunting caribou like other Eskimos. So they were put here at Prince River to fish for a living. Now, on top of everything else, they've got hepatitis. ..." He shook his head and turned towards the policemen who were chivvying people out of the tents preparatory to herding them aboard the canoes.

The two tents had held the remnants of five families, fifteen people in all. For weeks they had been existing on the scanty catch from two nets set at the river's mouth, a few ptarmigan and gulls, what berries the women and children could garner on the hills, and an issue of flour and some other staples provided by the police. Only three of their dogs remained alive, and these were in pitiable condition.

The eldest among them was a woman who looked as if she might have been a century old; she was little more than a bundle of mahogany hide topped by a wild fringe of thin grey hair. Tattoos, something that had long been out of fashion in most of the Arctic, were visible on her deep-wrinkled face. She possessed a radiant, if toothless, smile.

The policemen were having difficulty getting these destitute people to abandon their camp—until Doug said something to the old woman in her own tongue. She stared hard at him for a moment, spat, then, turning to her people, shouted a few words.

"They'll go now," Wilkinson informed the police. In an aside to me he added, "She told them they'd be fed if they went. But I think the old girl herself would sooner stay right here and starve."

Corporal Wilson aggressively superintended the loading of the canoes with men, women, children, and their pitiable little bundles of possessions. The three remaining dogs were not taken aboard. Nor were the people allowed to salvage their nets. "Take too long, and they're worn out anyway," was the explanation offered.

The old woman was one of our passengers for the trip home. She brought with her a battered coffee can into which she spat gobs of bloody phlegm. At one point, when it appeared she had coughed up what was left of her ravaged lungs, she turned to me, grinned broadly, and waved an arm towards the passing shore in a gesture that said as clearly as words:

"Wonderful country!"

I nodded, but was unable to return her smile.

10 The Land

waited for Wilkinson to volunteer the story of what he and others
referred to as the Garry Lake disaster, but he seemed by no means
anxious to do so. Then one morning he offered to introduce me to a

priest of the Oblate Order who had been involved in the affair.

"Father Choque is senior man at the mission here. He's going off in his canoe to visit the Eskimo camps on the south shore of the lake and might be persuaded to take you along. Two guys can get to know each other pretty quick when they share grub and a tent. I think you and Choque might hit it off and you might learn a bit about Garry Lake and the Back River people from him."

Father Choque was not home when we visited the mission. We were received by Father Trinel, a ruby-lipped, round-faced young Québecois who agreed to pass on Doug's request that I be allowed to accompany his superior to the camps.

"Trinel's not what you'd call a first-line effective," Doug remarked later. "He was actually with the Garry Lake band last fall and was supposed to stay with them all winter. He didn't do it. So some people blame him for what happened. Now the poor chap wants out. I hear his bishop has banished him back to Cape Dorset, where there isn't a single Catholic convert and presumably he won't get into trouble."

Shortly after our visit Father Choque sent word he would take me along if I could be ready in an hour's time. I was twenty minutes early at the dock where his dilapidated canoe awaited.

Charles Choque turned out to be of my own age, lean, wiry, thin-faced, with a heron-like alertness about him. He was a long-time resident at Baker, having arrived there from France in 1946 soon after completing his novitiate in the Oblate Order.

He greeted me coolly, told me to throw my gear aboard, and with no further ado pushed off. An easterly wind was building to gale force and in no time at all we were both soaking wet as the mission's old nineteen-foot canoe, inadequately powered by a worn seven-horsepower kicker, was engulfed in spray.

We were lightly laden with a minimal quantity of food, a tent and sleeping bags, two ten-gallon drums of gas, and a large wooden crate full of empty bottles ranging from half-ounce to half-gallon capacity. The latter had been supplied by Caygill as containers for urine samples.

We also had a pilot, a twelve-year-old boy named Tikaija who was deaf. Nevertheless he was supposed to be our guide to the first camp, which Charles had not previously visited and of whose exact where-abouts he had only a vague notion. Doug had warned me about this: "Choque doesn't waste time or money on things of the world, like a compass or maps. He relies heavily on God, who, I must say, has looked after him pretty well so far."

Our route took us into a maze of sandbars lying off the mouth of the Thelon where we were in constant collisions with unseen shoals that were breaking white in the rising storm. Charles's skills as a mariner did not impress me.

The shoreline was low and obscure. The only landmark seemed to be a large hill in the distance to which our young pilot kept pointing with some urgency. I think he shared my doubts as to the competence of our skipper. The sun was setting and the wind had risen ominously before we made out a cluster of tents that appeared to be floating on troubled waters. This turned out to be Kikialiak, a fishing camp at the mouth of the Ihugliaktiak River, and our first port of call.

The camp consisted of six tents pitched on a low estuarine island, and a seventh on the mainland to the west of the river mouth. Most were small and much worn, some being little better than windbreaks. The exception was a fourteen-by-sixteen-foot wall tent—a princely pavilion compared to the tattered shelters surrounding it. It belonged to Kanayook, the paramount elder, or "camp boss" as such men were known by the traders.

Glad as we were to reach Kikialiak, it was an unprepossessing place. Garbage of all sorts littered the stony ground. The stench was palpable. The people who drifted to the shore to meet us, all women and chil-dren, were nearly as shabby and forlorn looking as their tents.

We hauled our canoe up above storm level and plodded up to Kanayook's tent, to find him lying naked on a pile of caribou hides. He looked to be about seventy and had a scraggly, goat-like beard, hardly any teeth, and a well-rounded belly.

Although a Roman Catholic convert, Kanayook did not have an exalted reputation. Doug had forewarned me about him: "He's an unre-generate old scoundrel who became an RC because the Anglicans wouldn't have him."

He greeted us warmly and we sat gingerly on the edge of his bed while a daughter made tea over a sheet-iron stove burning willow twigs. She served Kanayook first, giving him a quart-sized enamel mug full of a black brew on which floated a scum of caribou hairs. Charles and I were given lesser portions of the same. As I sipped I noted that the tent's furnishings included a broken gramophone, a broken hand-powered sewing machine, a chamber pot *sans* handle or lid, and an array of smoke-blackened cooking pots.

We talked until it was too dark to see except dimly by the glow of the little stove. Charles, who was fluent in Inuktitut, translated.

I learned that Kikialiak functioned as a sort of holding camp for wives and offspring of men who had been sent south to tuberculosis sanitaria. Women and older children fished for a living under Kanayook's seigneurial direction. They were responsible for feeding thirty or forty sled dogs belonging to white residents of Baker Lake, mainly the RCMP, and, of course, for feeding themselves. The six tents on the island sheltered six "sanitarium widows" and seven children, all of them members of Charles's flock. The lone tent on the mainland belonged to a woman and her baby son. Since this woman professed the Anglican faith she was literally and physically beyond the pale.

Kanayook was the only adult male in camp. His wife was currently in an Alberta sanitarium, as was his daughter's husband. However, according to Sandy Lunan, Kanayook suffered no marital deprivation. As the trader put it with, perhaps, a touch of envy: "With all they women about, that auld bugger's like to fuck hisself to death!"

Getting to Kikialiak had not been easy. Getting away proved even more difficult. Day after day an easterly gale churned the lake to foam and fury. Not only were we immobilized, but the women could not get to the nets strung across the river mouth. In consequence, dogs and people alike went hungry.

Charles and I were not much better off than the rest. He had brought along a bag of pilot biscuits, one can of jam, two cans of beans, some mouldy bacon, and several pounds of tea (for the delectation of his adherents), trusting in the Lord to provide for him locally. I had only had time to rustle up a few cartons of biscuits and some chocolate bars before our hurried departure. These rapidly vanished into the mouths of hungry children.

I was shadowed by Kanayook's grandson, Robert, a boy of eight who had only recently been returned to his mother and his people after two years at Clearwater Sanitarium. There he had been made much of by the staff, had learned English, and had forgotten much of his own tongue. He was a lost soul at Kikialiak. Avoiding the other children, he stuck as close to me and Charles as he could.

"He fears we might leave him behind," Charles explained. "On this trip I will pick up children of school age and take them back to Baker so they can be flown to the residential school at Chesterfield. Most don't wish to go, and their parents don't wish it either because they won't see each other again for nine or ten months. But Robert is anxious to go. He is already what you might call one of the new Eskimos, halfway between his own people and us. Kanayook much wants him to stay here and be *Inuk*. But he must go. That is the law."

Charles did not express an opinion pro or con the law, except to say with a smile, "If the children must go to school, then we make sure they at least get a good *Catholic* education."

The weather was dreadful. The gales brought lowering skies and bursts of icy rain. The tethered dogs lay in sodden lumps, noses under tails, waiting for fish that were not forthcoming. Initially, Charles spent the daylight hours holding masses in Kanayook's tent. "It is not so often these people come to church," he said wryly, "so I strike when, as you say, the iron is heated."

Most evenings he and I and the rest of the camp's human inhabitants gathered at Kanayook's for tea-drinking soirées during which the old man talked at length and with passionate nostalgia of the days when his people had lived along all the major lakes and rivers across the Barren Lands. I recorded many of his stories, some going back several generations. They were vignettes of times past.

"Once we were very many. *Omingmuk* [musk ox] and *Tuktu* were also very many. We were all strong together. There were no white men in the land even in my father's time and we lived as we pleased. In winter men such as Oolibuk and Pipkana and Akligjivik would drive their sleds loaded with skins all the way south to Stone Igloo [Churchill], then all the way back north to trade powder and shot to the Kidliermiut and the Netchilingmiut [Seal People] on the northern coast. They would be travelling for three or four months. And everywhere they went were people.

"Now *Omingmuk* is almost gone. *Tuktu* are few now. And there are not many of us left in the land. Yet in my father's time it is said there were people living on all the great rivers and lakes, so many of them that the *Itkilit* [Indians] were afraid to come into our country, but our men would travel into the forests as far south as Tuktoriaktuak [Reindeer Lake] and the Indians would keep out of their way.

"*Eeema*. It is all changed. Perhaps sometime soon there will be nobody in this land and then you *kablunait* will have it all for yourselves. What will you do with it then? Tell me that. You cannot live in it as we did. So what will you do with an empty land?"

Despite the weather I was enjoying my "Travels with Charley," who was proving to be a witty and amiable companion. True, he did attempt to put me in charge of collecting the urine samples, citing the somewhat specious excuse that *he* was already in charge of the holy water. When I proved balky, he made Kanayook his urinary deputy, much to the old man's delight.

Kanayook visited every tent and personally supervised the sampling. "He is a dirty old man," was Charles's comment. "I shall make him say fifty Hail Marys in atonement."

Two days of Charles's ministrations sufficed to satisfy everyone's appetite for religion. Thereafter, ignoring the weather, the women and children spent much of their time on long excursions into the tundra looking for berries.

Relieved of his professional obligations, Charles gave himself over to his one indulgence—fishing with a spinning rod. He was good at this and managed to supply the two of us with enough fish to keep our bellies quiet.

Sometimes I joined the people trekking across the sodden land. The berries we sought, chiefly cloudberries, were scarce but nobody cared. The children played endlessly, sometimes pretending to be *amorak*—wolves—stalking a caribou—which was usually me. The women took every opportunity to brew tea over tiny twig fires around which they sat and gossiped.

We had company. Ground squirrels—*siksik*—whistled at us from sandy eskers; arctic loons grunted overhead, sounding rather like airborne pigs. We met families of Canada geese that were flightless either because they were too young to fly or were in moult. Oldsquaw ducks gabbled on ponds, the muddy margins of which seethed with shorebirds frantically fattening up for the long migration that would take some of them as far south as the Argentine pampas.

Robert noted my interest in animals and busied himself collecting specimens for me, including an iridescent azure butterfly about as big as my fingernail, a zebra-striped hunting spider, a flightless young Lapland longspur, and a dumpy little lemming. If he was disappointed when I released these creatures instead of eating them, he was too polite to say so.

On raised beaches of what had anciently been an inland sea, we came upon the habitations of people of other times. These chiefly consisted of rings of large stones used to anchor the edges of skin tents, many of which were twenty feet and more in diameter. These lichen-encrusted stone circles shared the ancient beaches with grave cairns through whose interstices fragments of human bones could be seen.

On the crest of one high ridge, I came upon a semicircular stone wall about three feet high behind which hunters had once watched for caribou. They must have had time on their hands, for the enclosed space was littered with still-shiny flakes remaining from the manufacture of quartzite points, knives, scrapers, and other tools.

An archaeologist who examined some of these same sites a few years after my visit told me they testified to a human occupation reaching across at least three millennia.

But now the country was virtually empty, not only of people but also of what had once been their life's blood: *Tuktu*, the deer. The landscape was reticulated with deer trails scoured deep into bogs and etched into living rock, but of caribou themselves we saw none. According to Robert, only three had been seen that summer at Kikialiak and only one killed. "People eat it all one day. After, only fish to eat!"

One morning the sky cleared; the wind came westerly and blew hard enough to drive the mosquitoes into hiding. Charles and I borrowed Kanayook's .30-30 rifle and went caribou hunting. We walked many miles over rocky ridges, dry tundra, bogs, and grassy swales to reach a great, rocky buttress called Sugarloaf Mountain by whites, and Old Woman's Skull by the Inuit. From its crest we could view the plains undulating south and west for ten or fifteen miles, but they were void of larger animals. No caribou were visible where, at this season, there should have been thousands.

"Last autumn, the same," said Charles gloomily. "And last winter many people died because there was no deer. Maybe the deer are gone for good. If it is so, then the people are surely gone too."

It was late afternoon before we arrived back at camp empty-handed to find that hunger had given the women extra courage. They had launched a skiff in a partially successful effort to haul the nets. Shamed by this display of fortitude, Charles and I decided we ought to put to sea and continue our travels.

Having flung our gear into our canoe, we corralled two of the three children destined for Chesterfield but could not find Robert. He had been temporarily "disappeared" by Kanayook to a smaller island where he was supposed to remain till we had gone. But Robert waded shoulder-deep across the river to the main island and inveigled some women into taking him aboard the skiff and rowing after us. I saw them waving their oars and we put back. Robert was determining his own destiny.

"Not going live like Eskimo," he told us, shivering under a blanket in our canoe. "Gonna be white man now. You bet!"

Before the day ended he may well have had doubts as to the wisdom of that decision. Certainly no Inuk in his right mind would have set out just before sunset to attempt a thirty-mile traverse of a lake that had been subjected to gale winds for almost a week. *And* without knowledge of the route, landfalls to be sought, or perils to be avoided, relying on an engine that was small, old, and badly maintained.

Before we had gone a mile, I knew we had made a mistake. The chop resulting from storms blowing in different directions almost literally stood the canoe on end. The boys and I were kept busy bailing while Charles tried to keep the engine from being drowned. Time after time a wave would short the spark plug and the canoe would roll into the troughs while Charles hauled on the starter cord until the veins stood out on his forehead.

We should have put back, but would not do so under the eyes of the women, let alone of Kanayook. Grimly we pressed on. Hours later we gained some shelter under the lee of an island, and just in time too, for we had used up all the gas in our ready can and had to refuel from one of the ten-gallon drums—a tricky business.

As darkness closed down we pounded on, by guess and by God as my grandfather would have said, with no idea where we were or where we might safely get ashore. Eventually, one of the boys spotted a *topay*—a tent—on the black horizon of what I had taken to be open water. Charles headed for it and soon we were thumping across a series of shoals to fetch up at last upon a windswept sand spit where four tents rattled and flapped in a chill wind.

We had landed near the mouth of the Kazan River, Keewatin's chief north-south waterway, and at a different kind of camp from the ones I had so far seen around Baker Lake. The large, well-kept, and sturdy tents were surrounded by an impressive accumulation of gear *en cache*, including robustly built dog sleds, good kayaks carefully lashed to a high rack built of driftwood, spare tents in canvas sacks, bundles of steel traps, sheet-iron stoves, ice chisels, and nameless wooden boxes burnished to the colour of old bone by wind and blown sand. All this gear awaited the coming of winter, which would pave the country with ice and snow and so enable people to travel overland by dog teams to their hunting grounds. Meanwhile, the men of this camp, accompanied by pack dogs, were ranging the plains far to the south searching for deer.

Their women welcomed us with gallons of tea, fresh-made bannock, and as much boiled char as we could eat. There was no shortage of food here nor, apparently, of anything else requisite to good living.

The tents were pitched on well-swept plywood floors. The one in which we ate was the domain of a rotund, middle-aged mother of two pretty daughters, and she ran a tight ship. The interior space was largely taken up by three neatly made wooden bedsteads and an assortment of cooking gear and dishes, all neatly washed and stacked. Two Primus stoves, a pair of coal oil lamps, and a gleaming little sewing machine produced a sense of well-ordered comfort that made me feel uncouth and dirty.

"What goes on here?" I asked Charles. "How come these folk are so well fixed?"

He gave me an embarrassed little grin. "What goes on is ... we are in the wrong camp. These are Harvaktormiut—mostly Protestants. They live along the lower Kazan River. They tell me the Haningaiormiut from Back River, the people I am looking for, are some miles to the east. We will go to them in the morning."

Although we had had an exhausting day, neither of us was ready for sleep. I found myself puzzling over the enormous differences between the camps we had visited. What lay behind these variations? I begged Charles to enlighten me.

Perhaps because we had now shared some adventures together, or perhaps because he had been bottling things up too long, he talked a little about the Back River people. He spoke briefly of their relationship with his church and then, at greater length, about an enigmatic priest named Father Buliard, who, as we will see, played a major role in their story.

The dawn of a wonderful morning sent the two of us on our way along a shadowy coast. Since we were almost out of food we left the boys in the care of the hospitable Harvaktormiut, expecting to return for them in a day or two.

Now the weather atoned for the grey bluster of the preceding week. The air had the clarity but not the chill of crystal. Horizons seemed to withdraw into infinity. There was enough wind to keep the mosquitoes at bay but not enough to impede our progress.

What did impede us were legions of sandbars. Half an hour after our departure we were hopelessly lost in the labyrinth of the Kazan delta—a maze of islets and obscure points of land offering no points of reference. We became more and more entangled until there was not enough water to permit using the engine and we were sometimes forced to go overboard and wade, towing the canoe behind us.

We began to enjoy ourselves. We took off most of our clothes and the sun burned our pallid bodies while the breeze cooled us. Eventually the water deepened and the rivulets we were following widened until we found ourselves in one of the main channels of the Kazan. We went ashore, gathered a pile of dwarf birch branches for a fire, and happily brewed tea.

Charles, gazing fixedly upstream, seemed abstracted.

"You know, my friend, I would much like to travel up this river. It is a truly great one."

"That it is. Years ago I was on its headwaters with the Ihalmiut. They call it *Inuit Ku*—River of Men. Five hundred miles long, or thereabouts, it runs through the Barren Lands from forest country right to Baker."

"Perhaps," suggested Charles a little hesitantly, "we *could* travel up it for a while. It is said to be a wonderful fishing river, and we could use some fish, eh?"

This was a surprise. Father Choque, the paragon of responsibility and dedication to duty, suggesting we play hooky? I caught an almost childlike eagerness in his expression.

"We could do that. Why not? Let's give it a go."

Alas, it was not to be.

At that moment we heard a distant thrumming. When I looked lakeward through my binoculars, I saw a big canoe racing across the mouth of the main channel. It slowed ... stopped ... then came straight towards us. We had been discovered.

It turned out to be Wilkinson's canoe, crewed by Atungalik and his brother. They had been sent to find out "what," in Doug's words, "the hell had happened to the pair of you, and to bring back the bodies if need be."

Like truant schoolboys we followed Atungalik out of the river mouth and several miles eastward along the coast to find the Back River people we were seeking.

Their camp was in grim contrast to that of the Harvaktormiut. The dirt floors of the five tents were strewn with fish bones and offal. The furniture consisted of old and almost-bald caribou hides, a scattering of battered tin pots, and a few splintered wooden crates. The only food was fish and there was none too much of that. Supplies of flour and lard issued as destitute relief supplies had long since run out. The only alternative to fish was birds, and the site was adrift in gull and ptarmigan feathers, mostly from fledglings.

This was a poverty camp, harbouring not only poverty of the flesh but of the spirit. The mood seemed to be one of passivity bordering on hopelessness. The people reminded me uncomfortably of a group of recently freed Russian slave labourers my regiment had encountered in Germany in 1945.

Men were absent from this camp—but they were not out on the land hunting caribou. They had been taken to Baker Lake settlement to work as labourers and as stevedores unloading the *Federal Trader*. They had already been gone a month and some of their women believed the men would never return. Charles did his best to reassure the women, but I could not tell how far he was successful.

While Atungalik and his brother collected urine samples, we had tea with a crowd of women and children. *Our* tea and *our* handful of biscuits. These people had none of either.

The kids, at least, seemed lively. Some of them had constructed a model of Baker Lake settlement on a sandy beach. It had an airstrip, roads, a radio tower (made from the tine of a caribou antler), and house enclosures outlined with small stones. I concluded that these youngsters were anxious to leap from their world into ours.

The mothers seemed more than willing—even desperate—to send their children away from home to school in distant Chesterfield Inlet.

I was impressed by this apparent passion for schooling until Charles explained that the mothers were not so much motivated by the virtues of education as by the assurance that the children would be fed during the winter that loomed ahead.

Charles was supposed to bring in only children over six years of age but found himself forced to accept five-year-olds and one little girl who, I suspect, could not have been more than four. This child had been so close to death from starvation the previous spring that she could, or would, not speak. Her mother carried her to the shore and put her into our beached canoe even before we had made a move to launch it. Here she sat in her filthy remnant of a cotton dress, as limp as a rag doll and looking not unlike one. We covered her with a blanket, for the wind off the lake was chill enough to make us glad of our parkas.

The wind was rising so we did not linger. Since Atungalik's canoe was larger and faster, he was instructed to stop at the Harvaktormiut camp to pick up Robert and the other children. Meanwhile, Charles and I headed out of the estuary into the open lake. Our passengers were two small boys and three little girls huddled together under a tarpaulin that gave scant shelter as the canoe pitched heavily into a rising sea, sending icy spray over all of us.

Then the motor stopped. I paddled frantically to keep us from going broadside while Charles did things to the engine and—presumably—prayed. When the kicker caught, he turned back towards the land. Farther to the west we could catch glimpses of Atungalik's big canoe as it crested the waves. He, too, was heading for shelter. We got there first, beaching our canoe upon a barren shingle shore where Atungalik soon joined us.

It rained and blew too hard the rest of the day for us to move. The Inuit lay under a makeshift shelter constructed of canvas and caribou hides draped over Atungalik's upturned canoe. Charles and I scrunched inside his little travel tent, our sleeping bags laid out upon a polar bear hide to which he seemed singularly attached.

"I don't own many things," he explained somewhat apologetically. "But *Nanuk's* skin is special for me. A Back River man gave it to me two years ago, saying it would always keep me warm. Perhaps if he had kept it himself he would be alive now."

"How did he die?"

"Frozen to death last winter near Garry Lake. He and so many others. ..."

Charles's earlier reluctance to discuss the Back River disaster was dissipating. Until late in that sounding night he talked with surprising frankness about the affair.

"Some people say we Oblates were to blame, you know. They accuse our order of wishing to keep the Eskimos in a state of nature. Perhaps that is a little bit true, but it is only because we hope to keep them faithful to God's will. You see, there is the problem of whether such a primitive people can ever find a place in the civilized world. Perhaps they are like Adam and Eve and should be left peacefully in their Eden, for that is how their world seems to them. Some of us have wished very much to preserve the best of the old Eskimo ways ... to protect those people from the contamination of our world.

"Father Joseph Buliard was such a one. He was the shepherd of the Back River people. It was his conviction that they should continue to live apart as they had done since creation. That was what he wished to see them do. That is what he *tried* to help them do. ..."

11 Soldier of God

Joseph Buliard's birth squalls were heard in the French provincial town of Barboux as undertones to the martial thunder of marching feet. It was autumn, 1914, and the Great War was under way. Joseph's *petite bourgeoisie* parents were good patriots. It was not long before Joseph's father took up arms.

As a child, Joseph gloried in the memory of a father who had fought in a noble, almost sacred, cause. As he grew older he decided he, too, would be a soldier, but a soldier of God. When he was eighteen he travelled to Liège to attend the seminary of the missionary order of Les Pères Oblats de Marie-Immaculée. If, during his novitiate, he did not shine intellectually, he was at least notable for the dogged persistence that is the hallmark of an effective missionary. Eventually he was ordained in the Oblate Order and sent to northern Canada, which was one of the order's major mission fields.

When the second Great War erupted in September 1939, young Father Buliard was far away from France, a passenger aboard a nondescript little ship steaming into the eastern Arctic. The vessel was the Hudson's Bay Company's *Nascopie*, on her annual voyage north from Montreal to resupply the Company's trading posts and to bring back the wealth of fur they had amassed.

Because *Nascopie* was the only vessel to visit many of the eastern Arctic outposts (weather and ice permitting), she sometimes carried passengers who had no affiliation with the Company. These were generally government officials, including Royal Canadian Mounted Policemen posted to the Arctic, but could include both Anglican and Oblate missionaries. The former were generally welcomed aboard. The latter were not, because the Oblates held trading licences and were therefore in competition with the Company.

On September 19, *Nascopie* dropped anchor in Repulse Bay, near the northwest corner of Hudson Bay. In those days the "settlement" at Repulse consisted of a tidy HBC compound; the ramshackle Oblate mission of Father Henri, OMI; and very little else except when, two or three times a year, Inuit came to Repulse to trade and pitched tents or built snow houses nearby. Most natives traded with the Company, but the professing Catholics took their pelts to the priest and heard mass in his tarpaper-covered chapel.

Despite its unprepossessing appearance, the mission at Repulse was the engine behind a major drive to bring Roman Catholicism to the entire east-central Arctic. Individual missionaries fanned out from it as far afield as Igloolik, Pelly Bay, Thom Bay, even Gjoa Haven on King William Island distant almost four hundred miles. They mostly travelled by dog team and small boats to one-man bastions from which they waged war on Satan, paganism, and Protestantism. Equipped with little in the way of material possessions, but buoyed by fanatical devotion to the cause, they endured formidable hardships.

Father Joseph Buliard did not have the appearance of someone destined for such a life. At twenty-five, he weighed, according to the Hudson's Bay factor at Repulse, "about as much as a hungry dog." Scrawny and ungainly, he seemed doomed to blow away in the first real blizzard. He was also very shortsighted and forced to wear thick glasses.

Father Buliard passionately aspired to serve God in the front line, but first he had much to learn. Inuktitut did not come easily to him, and learning to live and travel in the country was an enormous challenge.

It was imperative that he know how to handle dogs. One of his early attempts to do so ended in disaster. Two months after arriving at Repulse, he drove a team onto thin ice and the sled broke through. By the time he managed to drag himself out, the dogs had bolted. When he staggered into the mission, it was with badly frozen hands and feet.

Father Henri did what he could, but gangrene set in and it appeared Buliard must lose his hands and probably his feet, if not his life. Fortunately the HBC post had a short-wave radio and, even more fortunately, the manager was able to contact one of the few aircraft then in the eastern Arctic. This ski-equipped Fokker made a daring midwinter flight north from Churchill to take Buliard out.

He was hospitalized for most of the remainder of that winter. Returning to Repulse early in the autumn of 1940, he spent almost a year recovering the use of his extremities. But ever afterwards his hands and feet remained especially susceptible to freezing.

His dedication seems only to have been strengthened by this ordeal. He began bombarding his superiors for permission "to go to the Caribou Eskimos, those poor pagans of the inland who have no priest to help and guide them."[1]

His seniors were understandably reluctant to let him attempt a major mission on his own, but eventually they gave him leave to try his hand at saving the souls of the handful of Inuit who traded to an HBC outpost on Wager Bay, a scimitar of salt water slicing into the Barrens between Repulse and Chesterfield Inlet.

The people who traded to Wager Bay were not truly Caribou Eskimos. They called themselves Utkuhilingmiut (People from the Soapstone Place) and lived mostly near the coast at Chantrey Inlet and along the lower reaches of the Back River about two hundred air miles northwest of the post at Wager Bay.

In November of 1942 a party of Utkuhilingmiut men drove their sleds into Wager and were amazed to find that the *kablunait* population there had doubled. Father Buliard had arrived by canoe just before freeze-up and was preparing to spend the winter in a tent banked with sod.

The resident trader was appalled. He thought the young priest was insane to believe he could survive raging blizzards and temperatures of sixty degrees below zero Fahrenheit with such inadequate shelter.

The Inuit from Chantrey Inlet also seem to have concluded that this, only the second *kablunak* most had ever met, was no normal being. They did not know enough about *kablunait* in general to decide whether he was sane or not but, taking no chances, they humoured him.

Buliard wrote, "Kamoka [the chief man] is a pagan with a good disposition towards our religion but his status is rather difficult as he has two wives, one of whom he has had for 25 years, the other for 12. However he is firmly resolved to straighten things out."

---

[1] This and following quotations are from Father Buliard's letters and journals, as printed in *Eskimo*, a periodical publication of the Vicariate of Keewatin.

Which was to say that Buliard was firmly resolved to straighten things out for him.

Kamoka paid a second visit to Wager in February. When he headed homeward he carried a passenger on his sled. Nearly perished of cold and hunger, Buliard had abandoned his snow-buried tent to throw himself on Kamoka's mercy. Fortunately for the priest the Inuit are a compassionate people.

Hampered by desperate weather, it took Kamoka three weeks to return to his home at Cockburn Bay at the bottom of Chantrey Inlet. By then dogs and men alike were verging on starvation.

Buliard wrote, "[I was] saved by four families at Cockburn Bay. ... [Afterwards] due to lack of dog food and the Eskimos refusal to take me here and there, I could not contact but half the population and I was very sad about it. ... They profess to be protestant but in fact are still pagans. Some are fanatics while others are well disposed toward me. ... I suffered much from the indifference shown by some toward our faith, and the hostility displayed by certain men: 'What did you come here for? Go back where you came from!' but I stayed."

Being totally dependent on the Inuit for food, clothing, shelter, and transportation, he had no real option but to stay. The Inuit, on the other hand, had an option. They could have turned him out to fend for himself. To their credit, they did not do so.

At that time there were only two major missionary organizations in the eastern Arctic: Anglicans and the Roman Catholic Oblates. They operated in fundamentally different ways. The Anglicans actively co-operated with traders and generally lived adjacent to trading posts. Normally they were well supplied with food, fuel, and other neces-saries brought to them by vessels belonging to the trading companies. Rather than go "chasing after the natives," as one of them put it, Anglican missionaries concentrated their efforts on those Inuit who came into the settlements to trade.

Oblate missions, on the other hand, tended to be tiny, makeshift, and minimally supplied. Oblate priests were expected to make do with local materials supplemented by whatever the profits from their trade with the Inuit allowed them to buy. Their supplies usually came north by schooner, a haphazard arrangement at best, but the Oblates did things the hard way. It was a matter of pride with them to claim that, for the most part, their missionaries lived off the country.

In reality it was not that simple. Few if any missionaries were sufficiently expert hunters to be able to live off the country by their own efforts. The truth was that most Oblates lived off the *people* of the country.

They saw nothing reprehensible in doing so. As one Oblate wrote, "We dedicate our lives to bringing these poor savages into the light of the Lord. We bring them salvation. We feed their souls with God's words. Is it so much to ask that they should feed us when it is within their means?"

Early in May of 1942 Buliard's Inuit hosts brought him back to Wager. According to the post manager, they were greatly relieved to be rid of him.

Since there were no other natives in the vicinity able or willing to support the missionary and since the HBC factor was not about to become his benefactor, the young priest had to return to Repulse Bay.

It was not a triumphal return. He had made no converts, nor had he been able to establish a "foundation" in new territory. Nevertheless, he was not discouraged.

"If I am allowed to go back I shall do so even at the loss of my hands or even my life, for it is for God and there is no hesitation whatever."

Two years were to pass before he was given a second chance. In the spring of 1944 his superiors sent him to Baker Lake with what amounted to a roving commission. He was to contact various "pagan" groups of Caribou Eskimos and ascertain which might be most productive of converts.

Baker Lake in 1944 was, and had been for almost twenty years, Anglican territory. The newly established Oblate mission, to which Buliard was attached, could claim less than a dozen Inuit converts. Buliard determined to rectify this. He spent the summer, fall, and early winter of 1944 travelling with one of the "mission natives" by canoe and dog team west to the Akilingmiut along the Thelon River, and south to the Harvaktormiut along the lower Kazan.

The Inuit he encountered brought him no joy.

"They are a poor sort of people; slow in learning; hard to convince; of very feeble faith—all of which results from their ignorance, or their ancestry overcast with sorcery or evil practices. But it is for these 'paupers' that we have come."

During a long winter spent at Baker Lake, where he felt spiritually besieged by a largely Anglican population, Buliard brooded. He became convinced that his best hope of success lay to the north and west in the Back River country with a people called Haningaiormiut, of whom he had heard while at Chantrey Inlet.

The Haningaiormiut constituted one of two remaining groups of Caribou Eskimos (the other being the Ihalmiut) who had remained relatively independent of traders, missions, or government. The Ihalmiut were too distant to be within Buliard's reach, but the Haningaiormiut lived less than two hundred miles away to the northwest of Baker. Furthermore, a few of them traded there. Buliard, who was now reasonably proficient in Inuktitut, met some of these and struck up a friendship with one of them.

Heavy-set and beetle-browed, thirty-five-year-old Korshut was something of an anomaly amongst the communally oriented Inuit. His considerable energies and intelligence were generally directed to his own advantage, with very little regard for the well-being of his fellows. In the words of one of the traders, "He would have made a hell of a successful businessman."

Korshut seems to have sensed a rare opportunity in Father Buliard. Within a month of their first meeting, he asked to be accepted into the Roman Catholic Church. The overjoyed young priest apparently had no doubts about the Inuk's sincerity. He was quick to enlist the new catechumen to be his guide and mentor on a reconnaissance to the Back River people.

The two set out in early April of 1945 driving Korshut's team. After visiting a number of Haningaiormiut camps around Garry Lake (the largest lake on the upper reaches of the Back), they descended the frozen river almost to Chantrey Inlet, where an unexpectedly early thaw caught them and forced a hurried retreat to Baker Lake.

Nevertheless, Buliard felt the venture had been a great success. He had found his chosen people. It only remained for him to plant a mission amongst them.

He intended to go north again early in the winter of 1946–47, but this was not to be. The caribou had failed to appear in any numbers the previous autumn, and a consequent shortage of food for people and dogs alike determined Korshut not to risk journeying to Baker Lake, where Buliard awaited him with mounting impatience.

At the end of January 1947, the priest decided to wait no longer. He set out to make his own way north, accompanied by an unnamed "mission native."

Unsure of the route, the pair headed up the Thelon hoping to find a guide to Garry Lake among the Akilingmiut. What they found was nearly a hundred people at Aberdeen Lake surviving a meat shortage by fishing.

Buliard hoped they might be ripe for conversion. He was disappointed.

"They are quite willing to join the Church," he wrote, "but are delayed by 'others'"—a not-so-subtle reference to an overwhelming Anglican influence.

Nor were the Akilingmiut prepared to guide the priest to Back River. They knew (if he did not) that a diet consisting solely of fish cannot be relied upon to sustain men or dogs. And there was nothing else but fish in the Akilingmiut camps.

Courageously (or foolhardily), Buliard determined to continue on his way without their help. How he and his companion managed to do so is unrecorded, but by the time they arrived at Garry Lake they and their dogs were starving.

The Haningaiormiut were in equally bad shape; in fact, some had starved to death. The remainder were fishing for their lives at the narrows between Garry and Pelly Lakes. They had no food to spare, which was a severe disappointment to Buliard who had counted on obtaining enough fish from them to fuel a journey to the mouth of Back River to visit "a Christian family living without any moral support."

This was the family of the same Kamoka who had befriended the priest at Wager Inlet three years earlier. Having obeyed instructions to rid himself of his second wife, Kamoka had been admitted to the Church as a catechumen. Buliard was most anxious to complete the conversion, but the Garry Lake people could spare him no food for himself or his dogs. Not even Korshut could provide fish for the journey. Buliard and his companion were once more forced to return to Baker Lake.

In May Buliard made another attempt to reach Kamoka. This time he found a guide who knew the way directly north from Baker to Franklin Lake on the lower reaches of the Back. Arriving at Kamoka's camp and finding it in the grip of famine, the priest concluded that the inhabitants had been truly blessed by God in having survived long enough to be baptized.

These were amongst Buliard's first conversions and were of great significance to him. Perhaps equally important was the beginning of what became a powerful and enduring relationship between him and one of Kamoka's sons, an attractive nine-year-old whom the Father christened Manuel—Manueralik in Inuktitut.

During the next twelve months the priest made several unsuccessful efforts to establish a foundation amongst the Haningaiormiut. These failed primarily because of the difficulty of getting supplies into the region. Buliard's inability to overcome the problem of inaccessibility seemed to cool Korshut's initial ardour. Without a plentiful supply of white man's goods, the Inuk was not as helpful to Buliard as he might have been.

The strain of being forever cold, hungry, physically exhausted, and denied spiritual successes began to tell on Buliard. So much so that, in the summer of 1948, his bishop ordered him to take a leave of absence and go home to France.

He did not go willingly, pleading unsuccessfully to be allowed to remain on duty, for he was adamantly determined to plant a mission at Back River whatever the cost.

What he had in mind was not just another outpost. He had now been in the field as a soldier of God for almost ten years during which time he had effected only a handful of real conversions. Mulling the matter over, he had come to believe that his lack of success was principally due to the pernicious influence of other white men, especially traders, Protestant missionaries, and non-Catholic government officials. These, even more than pagan shamans ("sorcerers," Buliard always called them), seemed to him to be his principal adversaries. He had concluded that the only way to nullify these "evil influences" was to establish an Eskimo-only enclave in a region remote from white men. There, so he believed, Catholicism would flourish and, with God's will, reach out to embrace Eskimos elsewhere.

The idea was not original. Something of the kind was already being tried at the remote little community of Pelly Bay, where Father Vandevelde, another of the redoubtable Father Henri's protégés, was trying to establish a pale within which a group of coastal Inuit could be isolated from the influence of other white men.

Buliard intended to do likewise at Garry Lake. During his leave in France he obtained support from the leaders of his order. When he returned to Canada in late August, it was to find his own vicariate had acquired a new instrument that could materially advance his purpose.

Difficulties in transporting supplies and people to remote missions had always bedevilled the Oblates. In 1948 the Vicariate of Hudson Bay, whose headquarters had been moved from Chesterfield to Churchill, took a bold step towards solving the problem by establishing its very own airline, appropriately named Arctic Wings.

Arctic Wings had only one aircraft—an aging Norseman flown by a young man named Gunnar Ingebritson. In addition to servicing Oblate missions, Gunnar gladly accepted outside work. In fact, one of his early engagements was to fly me and my partner into the Ihalmiut country in May of 1948.

In September of the previous year, Ingebritson had flown Father Buliard and a load of supplies to Garry Lake, landing them at Korshut's camp near the narrows. At long last Buliard was able to begin his "beautiful task of winning over to Christ these ignorant tribes, uprooting their hard and depressing paganism to replace it by a consoling and revivifying religion."

He moved in with Korshut, who was camp boss of several families. Korshut had been instrumental in bringing Buliard to the Back River country. Now he became indispensable, not only in practical ways but through his considerable influence amongst the Haningaiormiut. Further, he provided Buliard with the nearest approach the priest had to a friend and confidant in the region. The truth was that the Father felt little warmth for, or affinity with, the generality of the people he was trying to bring to God. He wrote of them:

"They do not have a pleasant appearance and at times are even repulsive. ... They sorely need the missionary to drive away the dark clouds of paganism and show them the way to Heaven."

Buliard now determined to visit every Inuit camp east and north from Garry Lake to Chantrey Inlet, then west along 150 miles of coastline to the mouth of Perry River. In the process he planned to ferret out all who might be receptive to his vision, and persuade them to follow him to Garry Lake.

His companion on this ambitious journey was Korshut, in a multiple role as dog driver, travel guide, interpreter, go-between ... and recipient of a goodly share of the supplies Buliard had brought with him in the Norseman.

As soon as conditions for sled travel allowed, the two men set off for the mouth of Perry River on the Arctic coast, where a native trader had a small post. Buliard described the coastal people as being nominally "Protestant [Anglican] but thoroughly pagan at heart; immorality, theft and superstition being prevalent among them."

He and Korshut were well treated at Perry River, especially by a camp boss named Tomalik. Nevertheless, while generous with food and lodging, Tomalik was not receptive to Buliard's overtures. His recalcitrance kindled the Father's ire.

"It is not unusual to be confronted with such refusals. However I know that some day God's grace will change the obstinate heart of a man [Tomalik] rumoured to have committed murder. He is a leading sorcerer. His reputation as a thief is well established and he is feared by all the natives in the vicinity."

Travelling east along the Arctic coast the two men came to a camp on Johnston River. "Unfortunately these people would not feed us, neither us nor our dogs. I had to leave. ... I do not think that gratitude is a predominant character among the Eskimos; they often fail to appreciate the efforts and sacrifices we make for them."

Things got worse. Near Sherman Inlet, Buliard "found four families of real pagans in heart and action. ... I was greeted with undisguised hostility. ... In place of God recourse to the demon was practised. ... The children alone were sympathetic to me. Alas, the grossness of their language and their manners betrayed only too well the environment in which they were being reared. My reception is very bad. ... Contrary to Eskimo hospitality the people do not even offer me anything to eat."

As the pair turned south down Chantrey Inlet, they and their dogs were suffering severely from cold and malnutrition. They almost perished during a fierce mid-December blizzard, but were saved by a pagan family who took them in and shared scarce food with them.

Terrible weather and chronic hunger took their toll of men and dogs as they laboured southward on the ice of Back River. Buliard's tender hands and feet began to freeze. By January 12, when they finally regained Korshut's camp, the priest's survival seemed doubtful.

Fortunately, gangrene did not reappear. Korshut dispatched a sled and driver to Baker Lake with a message from Buliard asking for help for himself and for "the starving people."

On March 24 Ingebritson landed his Norseman at Garry Lake, bringing half a ton of government-issue supplies that were placed in Korshut's care. Buliard was flown to hospital in Churchill.

The priest had survived an extraordinarily hard winter during which he had travelled almost a thousand miles by dog sled through a hungry, unforgiving land. Although he had made no converts, he could solace himself with the hope that he had sown seed that might sprout in the years ahead.

By June he was back at the Baker Lake mission making preparations for a return to Garry Lake. In his journal he complained that, apart from his own colleagues, he was unwelcome at Baker. The reasons why were not far to seek. The Anglicans regarded him as a soul poacher. Sandy Lunan was outraged that Buliard had been given a trading licence, thereby depriving the HBC of the Back River trade. The corporal in charge of the RCMP detachment viewed the priest's activities as a threat to the stability of the social structure. There was even talk of trying to prevent him from returning to Back River.

Buliard pressed ahead with his plans. In July, when the ice on the northern lakes had melted and planes could operate on floats, Arctic Wings landed the priest and a carpenter at the site Buliard had chosen for his mission station—a small island a few miles to the east of the Garry Lake Narrows.

His reasons for selecting this place remain obscure. Fishing in the vicinity was poor. Migrating caribou seldom if ever visited the island. For several weeks during break-up and freeze-up it was cut off from the mainland. A bleak, bald little lump of rock, it offered no fuel and little shelter. Nevertheless, Buliard chose it as the centre of his universe.

Father Choque had his own ideas as to why. "You must know that Joseph was superstitious in some ways. He truly believed the country was full of evil spirits, Satan's tools, that were fighting him. Maybe he built on the island to make, how you might say, a little fort?"

It is as good an explanation as any.

Ingebritson brought in two more loads including a canoe and kicker, and basic supplies for the winter ahead. Then he flew the carpenter out to Churchill leaving Buliard alone in his new home.

A frame structure only sixteen feet long by twelve wide, sheathed in tarpaper, the mission was an insignificant blemish in that vast and lonely landscape. Furnishings were spartan: a narrow camp bed, a small sheet-iron stove, a rough corner table, a bench, a hand-made chair, and a few shelves. Because of the shortage of fuel, cooking was mostly done on a little kerosene-fuelled Primus stove. Although the cabin provided basic shelter, the interior temperature during winter seldom got much above freezing and, when blizzards blew, could slip well below.

Korshut continued in his role as grand vizier. Certainly he was very useful to the priest, but his awareness of his worth made him more demanding. Buliard had little choice but to pay up.

During the winter of 1949–50 Korshut again conducted Buliard on a tour of his "parish," which embraced some twenty thousand square miles of tundra between Back River and the Arctic coast, and a population of about three hundred Inuit.

This was another hard trip and, occasionally, a desperate one. Buliard spent some time at Lake Franklin with Kamoka, who, partly in consequence of his conversion, was enduring lean times.

"Two years ago," the priest noted, "his remaining wife died and since then he has lived alone with his children. ... They are not merely poor, they are faced continuously with the spectre of starvation." Buliard fails to add that without a woman's contribution an Inuit family could hardly hope to survive. In order to meet the demands of the church, Kamoka had divested himself of one wife. Now he had lost the other and he and the rest of his family were suffering the consequences.

Kamoka's son, Manueralik, now twelve, was a robust, open-faced lad much attached to Buliard, as was the priest to him. During this visit Buliard proposed that Manueralik come and live with him. It was agreed that this should happen in the autumn.[1]

In the spring of 1950 Buliard travelled to Baker Lake by dog team, bringing fox furs trapped by the Haningaiormiut and traded at his mission. Once more he found himself the focus of hostility. The Company accused him of stealing its trade. The Reverend James accused him of spreading lies about the Anglican faith. The RCMP were furious at his criticisms of their failure to investigate cases in

---

[1] Buliard was strongly in favour of Inuit residential schools. "At school you can train these good-hearted children to become strong and capable of resisting shamanism and immorality. You will bring forth clean living young people, pious, curbing their passions and resolved to live Christian lives without any pagan influence." Oddly enough, Manueralik was not sent to residential, or indeed to any, school.

which, according to the priest, his parishioners had been victimized by pagan ill-wishers. Buliard had written in the magazine *Eskimo*:

"I remember seeing an RCMP patrol depart from Baker for Garry Lake with plenty of dogs and a heavy load of fuel and food, and come back after some days without reaching its goal. ... Rarely if ever have they succeeded in making a patrol there."

When break-up released the frozen waters, the priest summoned Arctic Wings and flew north to what he expected would be the peace of his own little kingdom-in-the-making. He was in for a rude shock.

His refuge on mission island was no longer sacrosanct. During his absence it had been broken into and roughly used.

"My house was a mess. Everything mildewed; my flour a complete loss; my camp bed broken. They used up all my kerosene and took my shells. ..."

Although "they" are not identified, Buliard held Korshut at least partially accountable. "He could have stopped anybody even pagans from going in my house and robbing. Nobody would have gone there without his agreement."

Relations between Korshut and the priest were deteriorating. They would continue to do so at an accelerating pace.

At least some of the difficulties between the two men arose from the arrival of Manueralik at the mission in the autumn of 1951. A competent youth, he was soon providing services for the priest that Korshut had once provided. Whether because Korshut feared his influence was being undermined, or because he was himself enamoured of the lad, he became increasingly hostile. By the spring of 1952 he seems to have been actively stirring up trouble between Catholic families and pagan and Protestant ones. Moreover, Korshut began covertly taking the side of the pagans.

By 1953 Buliard's little theocracy still amounted to only nine families, all of them living around Garry Lake, although the priest claimed an additional thirty catechumens (mostly children) and twenty converts scattered across the remainder of his vast parish.

His adherents were a small minority of the population. What was worse, despite Buliard's most strenuous efforts, new converts were not being made and there was backsliding amongst those who professed the Faith. Moreover, the attitudes of pagans and Anglicans alike were hardening. The relative tolerance they had evinced towards the Father's attempts at building a little world apart were being replaced by active antipathy.

Some people at Baker Lake suspected Buliard's persistent and increasingly overt proselytizing efforts might be putting him in jeopardy.

In Sandy Lunan's words, "The native is not so easy to keep down as some folks think. You can push him about for a time and he'll smile and say nothing. But you can go too far. Then you'd best start looking over your shoulder."

There is no question but that Buliard was pushing very hard. He became more and more dictatorial in his dealings with converts and heathens alike. His behaviour seems to have disturbed at least some of his superiors, who twice recalled him from his mission (once for six months) nominally because of exhaustion. There seems to have been more to it than that. Some of his critics thought that, in the face of mounting resistance to his autocratic style, he might be losing touch. Others, more sympathetic, feared even his enormous faith was no longer capable of sustaining him.

On a bitter cold January day in 1954 Buliard and Manueralik unexpectedly arrived at Baker Lake by dog sled ... and remained there until mid-March.

No explanation was forthcoming as to why the priest absented himself from his mission for so long a time, but local Inuit heard from Manueralik that there was a famine at Garry Lake. It was said Buliard's people had stayed too close to the mission that autumn and had failed to kill enough caribou. For a time they had bought flour from the Father, paying for it with fox pelts. When that source of food was exhausted they had turned to fish ... only to find empty nets.

Then the Father went away.

During Buliard's absence two families starved to death at Garry Lake. And so did Kamoka and the remainder of his family at Franklin Lake.

In March Buliard flew back to his mission. His homecoming is described by another Oblate.

"Famine had raged during his absence and he found the house in a fearful state. 'Dirty, frosted, stinking, indescribable. All the locks broken, 600 frozen fish gone and many articles of value stolen; all the driftwood burnt, etc.'

"Instead of being grateful, those who had stolen spent their time spreading ill talk about him. ... But what caused him most suffering was these Eskimos resistance to grace. 'All they think about is drink, sex, dancing and eating.'"

No mention is made of Buliard finding the frozen body of one of his converts inside the door of the ravaged mission. An elderly man seeking aid for himself and his family had made his way there from a starvation camp ten miles distant, only to die in the empty mission.

Buliard and Manueralik restored the dank, foul-smelling hut to some semblance of livability but could not revitalize the priest's dream. Only four or five families now remained in the vicinity, and they were at least partially under Korshut's influence.

Korshut had become the power in the land. He seldom visited the mission any more, except to make demands, sometimes backed by threats. Buliard increasingly felt himself beleaguered by the land and its inhabitants.

Then, suddenly, the siege was lifted.

One summer day in 1954 a Canso aircraft landed on Pelly Lake twelve miles west of the mission island. It brought the first of many loads of materials for the construction of a refuelling and service depot for Spartan Airways, a company specializing in aerial photography. Spartan chose Pelly Lake as a temporary base largely because the company had been given to believe native labour would be available there to assist in the construction of a landing strip capable of handling multi-engined aircraft.

Doug Wilkinson described what followed.

"The airstrip had a tremendous effect, even though it only operated during summer months. Several of Buliard's people were hired to work on it. The Spartan staff—about half a dozen guys—were so impressed by the tough life Buliard led and by the hard-luck tales he told that they bent over backward to help him. They used to fly 'his' Eskimos in their Norseman out to where the caribou herds were, pick them up with their kills, and bring them back. If there was a medical emergency, they would fly sick natives out. When they left each fall they turned a big portion of their supplies over to the mission. From 1954 on, the mission lived from the airstrip, getting gasoline, stoves, fuel, food, you name it."

The bounty provided by Spartan accomplished what Buliard had failed to do: it drew people to Garry Lake from as far north as Pelly River and as far south as Baker Lake itself. The population burgeoned. Korshut's influence began to wane and Buliard's to be restored.

At the beginning of the winter of 1954–55 the priest was in high spirits. He and Manueralik travelled by dog sled through the northern reaches of his parish where he persuaded three Protestant families to come south and share in the bounty brought by Spartan. The Inuit are pre-eminently a practical people, so these and other newcomers experienced little difficulty in becoming at least nominal members of Buliard's flock.

Fortune continued to smile on the mission until the early summer of 1956. Then Manueralik became seriously ill. He had been ailing for a year or more, but now began coughing up frightening quantities of blood. There was nothing for it but to take him to the Spartan base, from where he was flown to Baker, thence to Churchill, and finally to a tuberculosis sanitarium in distant Alberta.

His departure had a shattering effect upon Father Buliard. For the rest of that summer he haunted the Spartan base, avid for news of his protégé. When, on September 16, the Spartan crew departed for the season, Buliard sent a letter with them to Father Choque at Baker Lake. It was brief, disjointed, and dispirited.

"He sounded fatigued and depressed," Choque remembered. "We hoped he would come to us for Christmas and take a little rest to make him more cheerful. We heard the police would fly to Garry Lake soon so we gave them a letter to Father inviting him to come."

On November 15 the bellicose roar of a radial engine reverberated across the glitter of Garry Lake. Minutes later an RCMP Otter's skis crunched to a halt close to the barren hump in a white plain that was the mission island. Because of the intense cold the pilot kept the engine running while two policemen muffled in heavy parkas climbed out and slugged through the drifts to the little black building.

No sled dogs howled a challenge as the men approached. No human voices raised a welcoming shout. The mission was empty, its floor lightly drifted with snow blown through a cracked window.

On the corner table lay a packet of letters, the top one addressed to Father Papion at the Baker Lake mission. The police exchanged this packet for one they had brought with them, then hurried back to the plane to offload supplies for the use of a dog patrol they were sched-uled to make later in the winter. Because they were apprehensive about the weather and anxious to regain the safety of Baker Lake be-fore darkness closed down, they made no attempt to contact any of the Haningaiormiut.

As the engine thundered for take-off, a man came running towards the plane from the mainland shore. He was only a few hundred yards distant when the Otter surged through a drift of snow and climbed away into the darkling southern sky.

It would be a long time before the police would hear what a man named Agdjuk had wanted to tell them.

Agdjuk had visited Father Buliard near the end of October, bringing fox pelts to trade for food. He had been dismayed when the Father told him there was nothing left to trade. However, the Father had made tea for them, then said a mass for his visitor.

Afterwards the priest began preparing his team for a trip to haul his nets, which were set beneath the ice at the narrows.

Agdjuk deferentially suggested that a blizzard might be in the offing.

"Father did not answer. He just drove off. Rest of day was much blowing snow, and Father did not come back to his house. I have no dogs so I stay there. Next day I look for tracks but snow falling too thick. Next day was big blizzard. Was four days after before good weather. Then I walk to place where one fishes, but Father not there and nets not hauled. Two weeks after, Father's dogs come into camp. We share them because that time we have no dogs left."

Ten days after Agdjuk's visit (and only three days before the RCMP Otter touched down at the mission island), a man named Teenak also made his way to Buliard's cabin. He entered without knocking and did not close the door behind him. Teenak was a baptized Catholic, but he had not wholly lost his fear of spirits.

The little room was dark, dank—and empty. Teenak stepped to the table upon which lay a small pile of letters addressed in feathery script to people and places beyond his ken. He hesitated, then, picking up the stub of a pencil, laboriously began writing syllabic symbols across one corner of the uppermost envelope. This done, he went away, gently closing the door behind him.

Two months later, a radio message from Gjoa Haven on King William Island was relayed through Churchill to Baker Lake. It came from the same Father Henri who had been Father Buliard's mentor at Repulse Bay. Henri reported rumours circulating amongst the Netchilingmiut to the effect that Father Buliard had disappeared the previous autumn and had not been seen since. Would Baker please investigate?

Corporal Wilson of the Baker RCMP detachment consulted Father Papion, who at first had nothing useful to offer. But then he remembered something. After some searching, he found an envelope containing a letter written by Father Buliard that had been picked up by the RCMP Otter on its visit to Garry Lake in mid-November. The letter was about routine church matters, but Papion recalled seeing an inscription pencilled in syllabics across the face of the envelope. Since he could not read syllabic script it had conveyed nothing to him. Now he wondered if it might not be worth a second look.

The inscription was succinct; it simply said: *The Father is missing.*

The authorities responded promptly. On January 16, 1957, the Police Otter arrived at Baker, took aboard Corporal Wilson and Doug Wilkinson, and was about to depart for Garry Lake when the engine began giving trouble. The problem proved to be minor, but those who fly over the Barrens do not take unnecessary chances. The pilot decided to return to Churchill for repairs, promising to be back in a day or two.

In the event, he was unable to make the attempt until more than a month had passed. And when, on February 20, he *did* take off from Churchill, he had to abort the flight because of a faulty variable-pitch propeller.

That night a frustrated Wilkinson wrote in his log:

"At this rate we are never going to get to Garry Lake!"

The NSO would gladly have made the journey himself by dog sled, but he had neither dogs nor sled. Since most of the local Inuit were dispersed to their winter camps, no native team was available. And the RCMP team could only be used by members of the force.

Wilkinson pressed Corporal Wilson to make a sled patrol, pointing out that he ought to be able to reach Garry Lake in a week or less, and could then make a thorough check of all the camps in the area.

The corporal's response was that this would not be necessary since the Otter would be along "any day."

"Any day" stretched into another six weeks.

Not until April 1 did the police plane return to Baker. At 9:00 the following morning it took off for Garry Lake carrying Wilson, Wilkinson, and Father Papion. Visibility was bad and the searchers saw no sign of life until nearly noon, when they spotted and landed near a cluster of snow houses at the narrows between Garry and Pelly Lakes.

One of these *iglus* belonged to Agdjuk. Now, at last, he told his story. Several others were also interrogated, but nobody appeared to know what had happened to the Father.

The police pilot had another job to do that day and was anxious to be on his way. After less than twenty minutes the Otter lifted off. It made a brief stop at the mission island so Father Papion could retrieve some of Buliard's papers.

Brief as the visit had been, Corporal Wilson had seen and heard enough to conclude that Father Buliard must have perished "by misadventure." This is how the matter rested.

Sandy Lunan had his own opinion.

"They's been more than one white man got foul of the natives back in the country and never was seen again," Sandy told me with a shake of his head. "Supposed to have fallen through the ice ... Aye, but nobody kens was they alive or dead when they went through."

Another Baker resident had this to offer:

"There's a popular idea that an Eskimo will always tell a white man what he thinks the *kablunak* wants to hear. Well, there's a good deal of truth in it. Corporal Wilson was in a hurry and wanted to close the case. I don't for a minute believe he got the whole story. *Was* it an accident? Korshut might be the right man to ask."

The final word belongs to Joseph Buliard himself.

In the course of his last visit to the Baker Lake mission, he had told Father Choque:

"Life has become very difficult for me at Garry Lake. ... Some day I may be found beneath the ice. ..."

12 The Snow Walker

Bishop Marc Lacroix, OMI, Apostolic Vicar for Hudson Bay, now had to decide whether to close the Garry Lake mission. He chose to keep it going under the aegis of young, diffident, and relatively inexperienced Father Trinel.

Trinel spent a few weeks at Baker learning what he could about the Back River people; then, on June 10, 1957, he got a ride to Garry Lake aboard a Spartan Norseman. He went with no very marked enthusiasm but at least did not have to go alone. Manueralik, who had returned from a sanitorium that spring, accompanied him.

Father Trinel chose not to move into Buliard's derelict hut. Understandably, the place gave him bad feelings. He and Manueralik pitched a tent some distance away.

Word that a Father had returned spread rapidly. Inuit began converging on the mission hoping the priest had brought trade goods with him. By the end of July nine families were camped on the little island.

They were not happy campers for they had counted on exchanging accumulated fox pelts for ammunition, flour, lard, baking powder, rolled oats, and other such goods. However, the Father had little or none of these things to spare, so the visiting Inuit had to subsist on fish.

The island was a poor place for fishing and the people had neither boats nor serviceable nets so Trinel loaned them the mission canoe and some nets. Even so they were unable to catch enough to feed themselves adequately. The young priest panicked and radioed an alarm via the Spartan base that "a community of sixty Eskimos" on mission island was starving and urgently in need of help.

"Everyone at Baker doubted this could be true," Wilkinson remembered. "Game conditions in interior Keewatin in August make it almost impossible to go hungry, let alone starve. Eskimos from other areas were reporting caribou. Corporal Wilson and I concluded the problem was that the Eskimos were staying close to the mission because of an inexperienced missionary. An experienced one would have sent them away to their normal summer camps and the problem would have vanished."

Nevertheless, the SOS was not ignored. On August 11 the police Otter picked Wilson up and flew him to the beleaguered mission island, where he spent a week distributing food purchased with the Haningaiormiut's own Family Allowance credits and hustling the natives "back to the land." Three weeks later he flew in again to ensure his orders had been obeyed. He also deposited a load of relief supplies in a storehouse at the Spartan base. Significantly, it was not Father Trinel but Manueralik whom he put in charge of this depot, with orders to issue food only in case of real need.

Meanwhile Wilkinson had been summoned to Ottawa for a Northern Service Officer's conference. At its conclusion he took his annual leave but instead of using the time for "rest and recreation" he set about making sure he would no longer be without some means of transportation in the region under his supervision. With his wife's concurrence he took their savings and bought a second-hand Piper Cub airplane.

"I knew it wouldn't get me everywhere I needed to go, the way a dog team could, but it would at least let me keep an eye on what was happening over a very big territory."

First he had to learn to fly. He did this so expeditiously that before his holiday was over he had earned his private pilot's licence. However, the little Cub still had to be prepared for Arctic flying, a time-consuming and expensive procedure that could not be completed by the time Wilkinson and his little family had to return to Baker.

Early in October the Spartan base closed down for the season. Trinel and Manueralik promptly abandoned the mission island in favour of one of the buildings at the airstrip. With Spartan playing fairy godmother, the two men were able to enjoy the luxury of oil-fired space heaters, plentiful and varied food, and comfortable surroundings.

The mission's parishioners were not so well served.

On December 10 Trinel and Manueralik arrived unexpectedly at Baker, having come from Garry Lake with a dog team driven by a man named Angotutuar. The priest reported that the Haningaiormiut had failed to get enough caribou, and that fishing was so poor the people were again on the verge of starvation. Some people, he said, had already killed and eaten their dogs.[1]

[1] Caribou were scarce almost everywhere in Keewatin that winter, but things were made worse for the Haningaiormiut by lack of the ammunition that ought to have been available from the mission but apparently was not.

Although Corporal Wilson was "doubtful that any real emergency existed," he radioed Churchill for an aircraft. The plane arrived on December 14, incidentally bringing Wilkinson and his family back to Baker.

Next day the corporal, the NSO, and Manueralik (Father Trinel declined to go along) flew in the police plane to the Spartan base at Pelly Lake. Nobody was on hand to greet them. Relief supplies consisting mainly of rolled oats, flour, and rice were unloaded. Manueralik could not be persuaded to remain here alone so Wilkinson wrote a note in syllabics and nailed it to the door. It was addressed to Teenak, head of a family believed to be living somewhere near at hand. The note instructed Teenak to take charge of the supplies and dole them out as needed.

A number of fox pelts, which Inuit had left at the storehouse in payment for food taken, were loaded aboard and the Otter departed. None of the Haningaiormiut had been met with, but the white men assumed the plane had been heard or seen by people who would deduce that food had been brought to the airstrip and act accordingly.

"We had done the best we could for the moment," Wilkinson recalled. "We had seen no indication of trouble, and Corporal Wilson had scheduled a sled patrol to the region within the next few weeks. In fact, part of the stuff we left at the airstrip was additional supplies so his patrol could travel about and check all the camps in the vicinity."

The autumn of 1957 at Garry Lake had begun ominously with the failure of the caribou to appear in their usual numbers and at the usual places. Almost none were speared at traditional river crossings. Hunters roaming the plains encountered few deer and were able to kill even fewer because they had almost no ammunition.

Before November drew to its white close, hunger had begun to haunt the fifteen snow houses scattered in groups of two or three around the shores of Pelly and Garry Lakes.

Fishing became the sole source of sustenance, but the ice was inexorably thickening and when people managed to chip holes through it, few fish came to their hooks. The last deer meat was eaten, and there were no more hides from which clothing could be made.

The deep-seeking chill of winter entered the snow houses. It also entered into sixty-two people who had no fat to burn in their lamps and precious little to burn in their bodies. The cold without was becoming the cold within.

As the long nights and short days of December drew down, some people fled the approach of the Snow Walker—the synonym for winter death. Iviok, a recent arrival at Garry Lake from farther north, was one such. He and his family hitched up their remaining dogs and travelled to Chantrey Inlet, from which place they could seek help at Gjoa Haven if need arose.

Eingidlik was another who saw what was coming. He took his family to the mouth of Johnston River on Queen Maude Gulf, where Netchilingmiut relatives of his wife made a good living hunting seals.

Two other men, Kreeyak and Ardjak, took their families into a hilly region north of Baker Lake, where, even in the worst years, some caribou were usually to be found.

Two of these four families were pagan; two were Anglican. None had faith in Father Trinel's ability to protect or provide for them.

When 1958 began, eight nominally Roman Catholic families, numbering in all forty-three men, women, and children, remained at or near Garry Lake.

Korshut's family and adherents were camped seven miles east of the mission island. The proximity of Korshut's camp may have been a factor in persuading Trinel to abandon the island and move to the airstrip, twelve miles farther to the west. Korshut's imperious demands unnerved the priest, as did the Inuk's increasingly open expressions of contempt for the faith he had once professed.

Three snow houses made up Korshut's camp. One sheltered the fifty-year-old hunter Angotutuar, his wife, and his two daughters. A second was occupied by twenty-one-year-old Arnaduak, his young wife, their two daughters, and Arnaduak's father, Iteroyuk.

The third and by far the largest *iglu* housed Korshut himself; his two wives; his father-in-law, Niakro; and two "adopted" boys. The latter were, in effect, hostages held by Korshut to ensure the submission of the families to which they belonged.

One early December day Manueralik walked from the airstrip to Korshut's camp. He entered Angotutuar's *iglu* bearing a message from Father Trinel. The Father had decided to go to Baker Lake and since he had no dogs, he wanted Angotutuar to drive him there.

The hunter was reluctant to leave his wife and two daughters at this time of famine, but twenty pounds of flour and a promise of as much food as he could carry home from Baker Lake persuaded him to go.

The journey took ten days. Having safely delivered Trinel and Manueralik to the Baker Lake mission, Angotutuar set out on his two-hundred-mile return journey. Luck was with him. He encountered a herd of ten caribou and killed nine of them. Jettisoning some of the flour and oatmeal given him at Baker, he piled his sled so high with meat that his dogs could hardly move the load.

Angotutuar brought home the wherewithal to feed Korshut's entire camp for a considerable time. But Korshut, who did not subscribe to the share-and-share-alike ethos of his fellows, took most of the meat and the bulk of the store food for his own use.

At this juncture, the families in the two smaller *iglus* moved into one in order to conserve what little fuel they had and what warmth could be produced by sharing their almost hairless sleeping robes.

By the end of January, Angotutuar's and Arnaduak's families had no more food. Appeals to Korshut having been rejected, they were forced to eat Angotutuar's dogs. However, these emaciated creatures could provide no lasting sustenance, and so the Snow Walker came into the *iglu*. His first victims were two little girls, one from each of the two families.

A few days later Arnaduak's father, Iteroyuk, informed the others that the time had come for him to walk upon the land. Wearing only a worn inner parka and a torn pair of canvas trousers, Iteroyuk went out into the long night. No trace of him was ever found.

Now Angotutuar made a last appeal to Korshut on behalf of his and Arnaduak's families. He was rebuffed. For some days he lay silent on the sleeping ledge, and then he died.

Soon afterwards Korshut came to that chill *iglu*, not as an angel of mercy, but to take away the dead man's wife and daughter. Korshut, it seemed, could not have enough women in his house.

Whether to make space for these new acquisitions or for some other reason, Korshut now told Niakro that no more food could be spared for an old man like him. So Niakro went into the night and walked upon the land.

On the north shore of the narrows between Garry and Pelly Lakes, a much-admired hunter named Kadluk had built a triple-domed snow house to shelter the nine members of his extended family. At fifty, Kadluk was one of the most effective of the Haningaiormiut, yet even he had been constrained to allow Korshut to adopt his youngest son.

Despite the shortage of caribou, Kadluk's camp did not, at first, go hungry. People worked together at the arduous task of setting nets under the ice and, for a time, were rewarded with sufficient fish to feed themselves and their few dogs. Kadluk and his two eldest sons, nineteen-year-old Akikunga (also known as Peewak) and fourteen-year-old Tuktituk, trapped white foxes whose pelts Kadluk took to the airstrip to exchange with Manueralik for flour, tea, and other staples. After the departure of Manueralik and Father Trinel, Kadluk still took what he needed from the storehouse, leaving behind the value in fox furs.

Others also took what they urgently required, but not all showed such restraint. In December Korshut made several trips to the airstrip, each time hauling away as much food as could be loaded on a large hand-sled. Teenak and some others followed suit so that by early January the storehouse stood virtually empty.

It was at about this time that the usually reliable winter run of fish at the narrows failed Kadluk and his dependants. The three oldest males desperately roamed the windswept Barrens, hoping against hope to find a caribou, a ptarmigan, anything edible. Or they crouched for endless hours over jigging holes cut through ice now six feet thick. They found no deer, few ptarmigan, and even fewer fish.

The time came when none of them retained sufficient strength to hunt or fish. Then, there being nothing else for it, they ate their skeletal dogs. When these had been consumed, they ate skin clothing and chewed fragments of old bones dug from under the snow.

The dying in Kadluk's camp began in late January. A four-year-old child was the first to go: his stomach and bowels so clogged with caribou hair and chips of broken bones that death must have been a release from torture.

By early February only four of Kadluk's people still had the strength, or sufficient clothing, to venture out of the triple igloo. One who was able to do so was Peewak, husband of eighteen-year-old Papaluk. Peewak determined to walk to the airstrip, eight miles distant across the lake, in the forlorn hope that a plane bringing food might have landed there.

With nothing to fuel him save a drink of water in which some fragments of deer skin had been soaked, and with his clothing in tatters, Peewak set out into a winter's dawn.

He was not the only one upon the lake that day.

Young Arnaduak from Korshut's camp could no longer endure watching his wife and remaining child perishing before his eyes, so he too set out towards the airstrip in search of a miracle.

So it came to pass that on a bitter February day two young men came by their separate ways to an unexpected meeting a mile or so from the airstrip. Their joy at seeing one another in the desolation of that time and place must surely have been intense, if indeed they were still able to feel emotions of that kind.

They walked the remaining distance side by side, the only members of their respective families who could have made this journey upon which rested the prospects for survival of eleven people.

As they approached the scatter of buildings, now almost buried beneath hard-packed drifts, they anxiously scanned the snow for ski marks signifying that an aircraft had recently landed.

They found no indications that any human beings other than themselves had come this way. Nervously they approached the storehouse, pushed open the door, and stepped into the dim interior. Upon the shelves and on the floor they found only some broken packages of tobacco and tea. There was nothing edible.

Frost crystals clung to the walls and windows: translucent butterflies forming intricate patterns of great beauty. These went unnoticed by two young men for whom the last ephemeral hope was gone.

They sat down in that almost empty room ... and waited. They could think of nothing else to do.

The long night closed in, crackling with cold. Arnaduak's torn skin boots had filled with snow, which had since melted. His feet were freezing so he took off the boots, together with his snow-caked trousers, and covered himself with pieces of cardboard cartons.

Although half-stupefied by hunger and exhaustion, Peewak nevertheless understood that without warmth both of them must perish.

How to get warm?

An empty five-pound bacon can lay on the floor. Peewak filled it with what he may have supposed was kerosene. Inserting a piece of rag to serve as a wick, he lit a match. ...

He had filled the can with aviation fuel.

A fireball exploded, setting the building alight and driving both young men out into the night. Peewak escaped wearing all his clothing, but Arnaduak fled the pyre barefooted and only half-clad.

The two young men crowded as close as they dared to the flames until these died down to hissing embers. Then they parted.

Using his freezing hands as clubs, Arnaduak broke into a bunkhouse to burrow under a pile of icy mattresses. There, presently, he froze to death.

Peewak fled onto the lake, and the ice boomed under him as he made his tortuous way back to Kadluk's camp. When he reached the big *iglu*, he found the Snow Walker had preceded him. His ten-year-old sister, Igupta, and his seven-year-old brother, Pungar, had joined the youngest boy in a shallow grave Kadluk had scratched in the snow of the sleeping ledge. The living now lay close above the dead, separated from them only by a single, parchment-thin caribou robe.

It grew very quiet in Kadluk's snow house in the days that followed. At length Peewak's young wife, Papaluk, could stand the silence no longer. She would not wait for death, she cried. She too would go walking on the land.

Luck was with her. Teenak, who was her brother, found her not far from his camp and took her in. So it was that one lived to tell the story of what had come to pass in Kadluk's camp.

No one lived to tell of the final days.

Peewak's starving body bloated obscenely, and then he died.

Kadluk himself went walking on the land. Perhaps he beheld a vision of gleaming metal wings; perhaps his failing heart sounded in his own ears like the distant throbbing of an aircraft engine. He went towards the airstrip, but never reached it.

There remained only his wife, Kabluk, her four-month-old daughter, Putalik, and her fourteen-year-old son, Tuktituk. One day Tuktituk stretched out a naked arm that had been reduced to bone and skin, clutched at the air, and his life ended.

Kabluk was now free to set out upon her own final journey. She did not walk towards the airstrip, nor towards other camps of her people. With Putalik on her back, she made her painful way across the ice towards Joseph Buliard's abandoned mission.

There is no way of knowing what was in her mind. Or how long that journey took her. There is no way of knowing when the baby died, but Kabluk had so little remaining strength that she was unable even to heap a protective mound of snow over the small naked body, so she left it on the surface of the ice.

Kabluk barely had strength enough to crawl through the open door of the mission hut. She died upon its floor. It is to be hoped she died without knowing that she shared that dismal tomb with the corpse of her son, Koonar, whom Korshut had "adopted" six months earlier.

During February food had grown scarce enough even in Korshut's *iglu* to make him decide that Koonar, and Sibiak, the other "adopted" five-year-old, should be fed no longer. Sibiak soon died, but Koonar clung stubbornly to life until one day Korshut put the emaciated and helpless child on a hand-sled and hauled him to the mission. There he had left the boy to perish—on Father Buliard's broken bed.

The *kablunait* at Baker had not forgotten about Garry Lake. On a number of occasions that winter Father Trinel talked of returning to his distant parish but never did so. And Corporal Wilson several times announced he was preparing a sled patrol to Garry Lake ... but somehow he never made a start.

On January 30 a very hungry man named Queenunhuk walked into Baker with the news that the caribou hunt at Aberdeen Lake had been a failure and that the Akilingmiut were famished.

Corporal Wilson summoned the police plane and flew to the camps at Aberdeen. There he did indeed find starving people. He issued half a ton of relief rations and flew one sick old woman out to hospital.

The RCMP's reaction to this emergency was both expeditious and admirable, but it was sullied by the failure to check on the situation at Garry Lake, only forty-five minutes' flying time to the north of Aberdeen. If the Akilingmiut were in trouble, surely it followed that the Haningaiormiut were probably in difficulties too.

The RCMP Otter flew south to Churchill, and Corporal Wilson reported to his superiors that he intended to make a sled patrol to Garry Lake and Back River within the next three weeks.

Wilkinson had his doubts about that. In fact, the patrol had not yet departed by February 26 when the NSO was called to Rankin to serve as justice of the peace in preliminary hearings into the Kikik case.

From Rankin he was sent to Churchill to deal with administrative matters. While there he shared with his superiors his apprehensions about the Haningaiormiut and his doubts that a police sled patrol would in fact take place. He asked for, and received, permission to go to Ottawa in order to retrieve his own little plane, in which he could fly himself to Garry Lake.

Between March 5 and 16 Wilkinson was in Ottawa fitting the Cub with skis, a more powerful radio, and survival equipment. On the seventeenth he took off on the long solo flight to Baker Lake.

In a consequence of what Wilkinson had reported, officials of his department had meanwhile conferred with the RCMP with the result that, on March 22, the police Otter was dispatched to fly Corporal Wilson to Garry Lake.

It was only after the Otter had landed near the Spartan base that Wilson realized the storehouse had vanished. He and another policeman scrabbled about in the drifts and uncovered some charred debris, but found no indication of why the building had burned or of what had happened to its contents.

Because the day was growing old, no investigation was undertaken. Neither was any contact made with the Haningaiormiut. After hurriedly offloading some seven hundred pounds of supplies the Otter headed home.

Next day Wilkinson's little Cub landed on the ice at Baker, having arrived just in time for him to help celebrate his daughter's birthday.

His relief at hearing that the RCMP had patrolled to Garry Lake, albeit by air, was tempered by the failure of the police to contact the Haningaiormiut. Wilkinson determined to go and see for himself how matters stood.

Unfortunately the weather was so bad during the next two weeks that he was unable to fly anywhere. Not until April 10 was the weather fit for a flight to Garry Lake, but by then he had received a radiogram instructing him to proceed to Rankin Inlet, to act as Prisoner's Friend at Kikik's trial. This new delay extended for another fourteen days.

Wilkinson's flight to the Haningaiormiut did not take place until April 24. Just after noon on that clear, cold day, the Cub, bearing Wilkinson and Corporal Wilson, finally touched down near the Spartan base. As it taxied to shore, Teenak came slowly out to meet it. Gaunt and exhausted, he was nevertheless smiling—as a man might who sees salvation come.

It was from Teenak that Wilkinson heard the first account of the tragedy that haunts him to this day.

As May came and the sun rose higher and grew stronger, birds began returning to the Barren Grounds. Gulls and a few red-throated loons appeared on a patch of water opened by swift-flowing currents at the Garry Lake Narrows.

The birds were not the only airborne arrivals.

Almost daily the hard blue skies shuddered to the sound of aircraft engines.

"They came like ravens to a caribou kill," one who was there grimly remembered. And, indeed, the stench of death hung so heavily over the land that it penetrated into the distant country of the *kablunait*, even so far away as Ottawa.

Policemen and government officials descended on the Haningaiormiut.

They brought food for the survivors.

They flew those in dire need of medical attention to southern hospitals.

They carried seventeen corpses back to Baker Lake to be autopsied.

The coroner's findings were that these seventeen Inuit had died because of "malnutrition and starvation."

Nothing was said about neglect.

Kadluk's camp was the last one to be examined. The entrance tunnel to the triple *iglu* was so solidly drifted in that the investigators had to break through the roof. The glare of sun and snow outside the house was so dazzling that at first they could see nothing in the chill gloom within. But after a while the light seemed to strengthen. And, they saw the naked, upraised arm of a boy reaching out for help that never came.

13 Travelling Men

The homeward-bound canoe bearing Father Choque and me back to Baker Lake made slow progress. The gale still blew as if it intended to do so until doomsday, and we had not gone many miles before high waves again forced us ashore. This time we landed on Orkpiktuk Island, a hump of tundra emerging from the lake not far west of the mouth of the Kazan.

The prospect of being weather-bound here, perhaps for several days, did not disturb Charles unduly.

"The grub box is empty," he noted after a quick look. "*Eh bien!* The Lord will provide."

With which he picked up his casting rod and set off along the foaming beach.

Not being a fisherman, I chose to borrow Atungalik's rifle and go inland. I found nothing of particular interest until I reached the eastern coast of the island. Here, at the foot of a protected little cove, I came upon the site of Baker Lake's first trading post, built by the HBC in 1913 at a place where for innumerable centuries people had been accustomed to camp while travelling the Thelon River–Baker Lake–Chesterfield Inlet waterway.

Detritus left by prehistoric men had accumulated along with that of their successors to produce a singular archaeological *mélange*. Bone and stone artefacts were intermingled with fragments of glass and china. Chipped quartzite blades, with green-patinated brass cartridge cases. Corroded bits of Primus stoves and pieces of defunct kickers, with bone slats and ivory sled runners. Rusted fragments of tin cans, with the crumbling ribs and vertebrae of caribou, musk ox, wolf, and fox. The great white skull of a Barren Lands grizzly jutted out of the moss not far from a human skull whose ancient grave mound had been opened by weather and scavengers.

Singularly impressive were the hulks of three cast-iron stoves. Seen from a distance, these resembled wreckage from some storm-lost ship. Brutally heavy and virtually impossible to keep supplied with fuel, such monstrosities had nevertheless served as status symbols to generations of Inuit until they went out of style in the 1930s, to lie abandoned across the width and breadth of the Arctic, an enduring testament to the ephemeral nature of human fashions.

There seemed to be no arctic hares or ptarmigan on the island, for which I was thankful since it meant I did not have to shoot anything. At one point I did surprise a family of sandhill cranes in a berry bog. The statuesque grey birds eyed me sternly, and one of them rattled a peremptory, machine-gun-like warning, at which I meekly withdrew.

On my return empty-handed to camp, I found several of the children conducting what seemed to be a bombing raid. They had built a number of small stone structures and, to the accompanying sound of aircraft engines, were dropping pebbles on them. I thought they were bombing a toy town, but mistook their intention. They were dropping food on a starving Inuit camp. ...

Charles had managed to catch one very small northern pike. Now Atungalik and his brother looked glumly at our hungry mob, then at the sky. The wind seemed to have dropped a bit and only one major open-water crossing remained between us and a string of islands that offered a sheltered passage the rest of the way to the settlement. What to do? The choice seemed to be a wet and risky venture at sea, or a hungry night in camp with the possibility that a new storm might pin us to Orkpiktuk for days to come.

The Inuit looked to Charles. He looked to heaven then glanced in my direction. "*Eh bien.* I will make some good prayers for travellers on the waters."

Emerging from the shelter of the island, we met the gale right in our teeth. Our canoe began to pitch and toss like a wild thing. It took the strenuous efforts of all of us bailing hard to keep abreast of the solid water coming in over the bow. The children, hungry and wet to the skin but bright-eyed and grinning, seemed to relish the whole affair. I did not. I knew that if the kicker failed we would almost certainly broach. Then it would be time to swim. It would be a short swim, for the water was paralytically cold.

The two canoes kept close together so we could come to each other's aid if need be. Four hours of hard punching got us across the big opening and into the shelter of the coastal islands. For a time the way was illuminated by a spectacular sunset filling the western sky with garish pyrotechnics. Then darkness came crashing down, and we felt our way across many shoals and reefs to a landing on the settlement beach.

An unsmiling NSO met us on the shore. He was accompanied by several women who took charge of the shivering children, herding them off to warm tents and huts. Wilkinson led Charles and me up to his achingly empty house, where I poured us all a drink of rum. Charles did not linger. He was anxious to get home where, in his absence, his favourite bitch had given birth to seven pups.

Doug was depressed and edgy. He told me the nurse had already identified five cases of hepatitis and believed many more were still to be diagnosed. Yet, despite urgent radio pleas, no help had come: no gamma globulin and no doctor.

Doug accompanied me to the nursing station to deliver the urine samples Charles and I had collected. Caygill informed me they were now so old as to be probably useless.

"Why didn't you get them in sooner?" he snapped. I held my tongue as Doug edged me out the door.

Wilkinson's mood did not improve overnight. It was a relief when, next morning, he strode off to the radio station to dispatch a peremptory message to Ottawa demanding immediate medical assistance.

I walked down to the shore to get some of my gear out of the canoe and found Atungalik overhauling his kicker. He greeted me as a fellow voyager and invited me to come to his house that afternoon and meet some of his friends.

As befitted the assistant to the NSO, Atungalik lived in a snug wooden cabin supplied with electricity. The kitchen boasted a chrome-and-plastic table-and-chair set, but the several Inuit gathered there were all sitting on the floor, backs to the wall, legs extended, and steaming mugs of tea beside them.

They were a motley group. Fifty-year-old Louis Tapetak was a famous hunter who had guided VIP sportsmen from the distant south on trophy hunts. At one time he had worked as a special constable for the RCMP. Then, he had signed on as "assistant cook" (scullery boy) aboard a small freighter and sailed in her to Newfoundland, and to Montreal, where he found himself stranded for the winter. He did not have a good time there.

"People think I Indian and treat me bad. Was in jail a lot, mostly 'cause I had nowhere to sleep. Was pretty near ready to walk home, when spring come and I got job on a northern supply boat."

Returning north, he honed his natural-born mechanical abilities and became a bulldozer driver with the DOT at Baker Lake. Louis Tapetak had been around.

Sitting next to Louis was a quaint little manikin lost in the folds of a huge sweater. His name was Parker and he was said to be well over eighty years of age. Parker chewed the willow stem of a hand-made soapstone pipe while interjecting a string of "eee ... eee ...eee"s (yes ... yes ... yes) into the flow of conversation, as if to add emphasis to what the speakers were saying.

Close beside Parker sat his current lady, bizarrely tattooed and ancient Toolik. Others present included Armand Tagoonak, the adopted son of the catechist at the Anglican mission. Armand's real father, an RCMP constable, had not been heard from since being posted back to southern Canada eighteen years earlier.

My intrusion temporarily put a damper on the gathering, but it was not long before I was accepted (or perhaps ignored), and talk resumed. Armand and Louis, both of whom spoke reasonably fluent English, interpreted for my benefit.

The mood was struck when, at my request, Louis asked Toolik how old she was. With a gaping grin, she claimed she couldn't possibly know, but maybe the police would have a record since they kept records of everything! This brought gales of laughter and a spate of stories about the police.

Old Parker remembered the time a police sergeant and constable travelled all the way from Chesterfield to Baker Lake by dog sled to arrest a man named Tooluktuk, who was supposed to have killed his brother in a fight over a woman.

"Tooluktuk say he don't do it, but police say they know better, so he got to go back with them to Chesterfield. On the way they lose the track and stay lost until Tooluktuk get hungry and show the way. When they get there, they put him in jail and say he got to stay until August, when the ship bring a magistrate and they can have a trial.

"Well, it's just past Christmas then, and Tooluktuk tell them he can't wait; his family need him. They keep him locked up just the same till one night is very bad blizzard. Nobody can see nothing. Tooluktuk go out a window. He hitches the police dogs to the big police *komatik*, then he piles it up with grub and ammunition and all kinds of stuff from the police storehouse and takes off.

"That's about 1925, and it's the last the police ever see of Tooluktuk. They look for him everywhere for years and years. He gone like a caribou. They don't find him because Tooluktuk drive back to Baker, pick up his wife and kids, and go to Tulemalu Lake two hundred mile southwest of Baker, and live there until he dies, an old man, older even than Parker. Everybody know all about him but the police never find him."

Louis Tapetak had a police story of his own.

"One time—1946 I think—a Catholic priest go crackers here. That Father been at Beverley Lake, living like a dog. People there couldn't stand the stink of his camp and couldn't eat the kind of stuff he did.

"After that he go up the Kazan and got worse. People there got scared, he was so crazy. Father Philip was in charge of the mission here, so he went into the country and got him and brought him out.

"Sergeant Jimmy was police boss here then. Very sour man. Never laugh or smile. He put that priest in jail—for his own protection, is what Jimmy say. Keep him locked up but let him go outside to pee. One night that priest go out and next thing he is in Sergeant Jimmy's house pulling the clothes off Mrs. Jimmy.

"About then Sakpeetna come by and hear the racket. He go tell Jimmy and he run up to his house and take the priest back to jail before he can get down to business with Mrs. Jimmy.

"Sakpeetna sorry after. He say everybody but Sergeant Jimmy be happier if he just walk the other way that night."

The ability of the Inuit to travel enormous distances across what some consider to be one of the harshest landscapes in the world has always fascinated me. What the Bedouin and their camels did in the desert, the Inuit and their dogs did in *their* country. Our tea talk had its share of stories about famous travellers. Parker particularly remembered Idjuatik.

"That fellow come from Hicoliguak [Yathkyed Lake]. Long time ago, when he still a boy, his father take him to Igluyarik [Churchill] and white people there take him on boat.

"That boat got wrecked in Labrador and Idjuatik come on shore and Indian people find him. They adopt him, but he want to see his own people so he start travelling west. In about a year he get back to Hicoliguak.

"After that he never stop travelling. One time he go west along Thelon, then north to Bathurst Inlet and spend summer with Kidliermiut catching white whales. Next winter he go on west to Coppermine, hunting *Omingmuk* [musk ox]. Next winter he come back to Kazan; gone for three years on that little trip.

"Was a very big [famous] man. Everybody know him. He is camp boss at Hicoliguak. But around 1930 something change him. He don't travel no more. He say *kablunait* making the land go rotten. So he live away off from them all the rest of his life—maybe twenty years—and never let his people go where white men are. Nobody live at Hicoliguak now. Only dead people now."

The names of other famous travellers surfaced: Tommy Atkins, Billy Brass (so named by white traders), and Shiniktuk (whom I had met at Rankin) were among them. In the late thirties this trio had been the Three Musketeers of the Barren Lands, travelling together seven hundred miles south from Queen Maude Gulf to Reindeer Lake (which lies deep inside Chipewyan Indian territory) and nine hundred miles east and west between Coral Harbour and Coronation Gulf. They did a bit of trading but for the most part travelled because that was what they liked to do, or perhaps sometimes because they had made things too hot for themselves at home.

Parker remembered the young Tommy Atkins as "a hell-raiser. One time at Chesterfield a priest catch Tommy looking in window of nuns' house and hit him on the head with big iron cross he carry around his neck.

"Tommy don't like that. He wait a while till bishop from Rome come north to meet Inuit people. Priests at Chesterfield going to have big mass for him.

"It early winter then and time for hunting polar bears along the coast. No bears come by yet, but everybody all the time looking for them. Well, all the people from all around Chesterfield go to church for special mass and the place is full right up. All of a sudden, door bangs open and Tommy busts in yelling, 'Nanuk! On harbour ice! Nanuk!'

"Two minutes after, is nobody in church except bishop, priests, and nuns.

"Funny thing, is no bear in harbour neither.

"That when Tommy decide he going to live with Billy Brass at Baker Lake."

Idjuatik was not the only one to reject the world of the *kablunait*. Toolik reminded her listeners of Shikshik, a powerful Harvaktormiut *angeokok* (shaman) from the lower Kazan.

"I see him do tent-shaking many times. His face turn black, his eyes stick out, then tent begin to shake and shake. By and by, big voices come from somewhere and all people in the tent crouch down. Then Shikshik spirit fly up to the sky and talk to other spirits. When he comes back he weak like baby and wet all over. One time he say bad time for caribou come that fall and we should catch all we can right now. So that's what we do. After October is no more caribou in the country, but we already got lots and eat good all winter."

Shikshik would not permit anyone who had been contaminated by the missions to live in his camp. Such was his influence that almost all the Harvaktormiut remained pagan until after his death in 1946.

Armand Tagoonak did not hold Shikshik's memory in high regard.

"It was the devil used to shake the tents, and tell lies to the people. Good thing those old *angeokoks* all gone now. God is the best protection."

Parker glanced sideways at Toolik and murmured, "*Imaha*." At which she nodded just perceptibly.

Imaha means "maybe."

Although assurances had been received that help to deal with the hepatitis outbreak was on the way, August was almost at an end before an aircraft from the south appeared.

The RCMP Otter CF-MPP roared in for a spectacular landing, then taxied to shore while half the community ran to meet it. But not everyone was in a hurry. Corporal Wilson and his wife came down to the beach at a leisurely pace, accompanied by half a dozen Inuit men laden with suitcases and roped-up boxes. The corporal was wearing a civilian suit and his wife a pretty little travel dress.

It was then we learned that the Otter had been sent to pick up Wilson and his wife and fly them south for their annual holiday, after which they would proceed to a new posting in another part of the north.

Doug was dumbfounded. Collaring the sergeant-pilot, he demanded to know whether MPP intended to fly to the out-camps to check on the hepatitis outbreak before returning south.

"Sorry, Doug. We've no orders to do that. Have to be back in Churchill tonight."

"Where the hell's the Department of Health doctor they were supposed to be sending in? And the medicines we asked for?"

"Sorry again. Nobody said a thing to me about a doctor. But some guy from DOH did give me a package for Caygill."

He handed over a carton containing one hundred milligrams of gamma globulin, enough for the initial treatment of two or three hepatitis sufferers.

In desperation, Doug turned to the departing corporal.

"Jesus, Don! We've *got* to visit the camps. *You* know what the situation is! We can't let the plane go south yet!"

The corporal was no help.

"It's none of your business, Wilkinson. Why is Northern Affairs mixing up in this anyway? It's a Department of Health matter." With which he turned and walked towards the waiting plane.

Whatever Doug might have intended to say or do, he was diverted by the appearance of a second Otter coming in to land. All of us were sure *this* plane would be the one bringing medical aid.

Not so. The new arrival was from Yellowknife, capital of the Northwest Territories. Instead of doctors and medicines, the second Otter had brought us the Northwest Territories Circuit Court.

The members of the court were unaware that a health crisis existed at Baker Lake. When told about it, they were concerned and sympathetic, but unable to offer assistance. The Crown prosecutor apologized to Wilkinson:

"Yellowknife won't authorize use of this plane for anything except judicial work without clearance from the justice department in Ottawa. You could try to reach them, though I doubt they'd want to get involved."

"They won't," Doug snarled furiously. "Nor will anyone else out there until a bunch more Eskimos die here."

With that, he strode off towards the radio station leaving me with a somewhat uneasy Crown prosecutor, defence attorney, court clerk, stenographer, and Judge Jack Sissons.

I was delighted with the opportunity to meet Sissons, a rather pudgy and ordinary-looking middle-aged man who was fast becoming legendary in the Arctic. Despite spirited opposition from the Old Empires, he was resolutely bringing a new concept of justice and a new practice of the law to the north. He explained to me:

"Our law must consider the legal beliefs of native peoples and take these into consideration when they come before the courts. Furthermore, it is absolutely imperative that we bring the courts to them in their own country, rather than whisk them away south to face our justice in places they know nothing about. There they are strangers in a foreign land, without a clue what is happening to them. No wonder they don't expect to get real justice at our hands. No wonder they call our justice cruel."

This was the same Jack Sissons who, earlier in the year, had presided at the trial of Kikik and had virtually instructed the jury to bring in a verdict of acquittal.

Sandy Lunan joined the group at the shore and invited us all back to his home for coffee. We were sitting around his hospitable kitchen table engaging in that favourite pastime of the north—gossiping—when we were interrupted, first by the roar of the police Otter taking off, then by the tempestuous arrival of the NSO.

Dark of face, he burst into the kitchen, grabbed Sandy's phone, and rang the radio station. In staccato fashion, he ordered the operator to recall the plane.

"Tell the sergeant it's a serious emergency. ... No, not medical. Criminal. Call me back as soon as you've talked to him."

We waited expectantly for an explanation, but one was not forth-coming. An ominous silence hung over the room until the phone rang. Doug jammed the receiver against his ear, grunted angrily, hung up, and charged out of the kitchen. As he passed behind my chair, I thought I heard him mutter, "Bastards!"

It was a while before I pieced together what had happened.

Apparently there had long been speculation in the white community about nurse Caygill's sexual preferences. Sandy Lunan, for one, had drawn conclusions from the fact that his handsome young clerk was spending most of his free time at the clinic-cum-nurse's residence. But nothing came of any of this until the day of Corporal Wilson's departure.

On that morning the Anglican catechist, Thomas Tapatik, nerved himself to tell Canon James something the Inuit of Baker Lake had known for half a year: that the nurse had been sexually abusing male patients, including children.

The first person the horrified Canon encountered after hearing Thomas's tale was Wilkinson. Almost incoherent, Canon James repeated what he had been told. Doug raced off to try to stop MPP, but the plane was already beginning its take-off run so he ran on to the detachment office and told the story to the constable in charge. Accompanied by an interpreter, the constable and the NSO then went to the Inuit community and began asking questions.

It took only a few minutes to establish that at least two incidents of buggery had taken place. It was at this juncture that Doug had tried to recall MPP.

When his attempt to do so failed, the NSO and the constable were left to deal with the matter on their own. By mid-afternoon they had uncovered six convincing accounts of sexual assault, at which point Doug, in his role as magistrate, instructed the policeman to arrest the nurse.

As the summer night closed down over Baker Lake, Caygill volunteered a confession. However, because he was the only person capable of looking after the hepatitis patients, he was not locked up.

"Hobson's choice," was how Doug put it when he returned home at last.

The anger that had been wrenching at his guts for the past several days seemed to have burned itself out. I poured the last of my bottle of rum into a mug and gave it to him. He sipped slowly, and for a long time was silent. When he spoke again it was with infinite sadness.

"You know, Farley, when I signed up as an NSO I really believed life for the Eskimos was going to improve. I felt I could do useful work to help that along. But in the past six months it seems everything's gone down the drain.

"Maybe it'll get better. Maybe the powers that be will smarten up. Maybe the Eskimos will get a grip on their lives again.

"I hope so. God, I hope so!

"But I'll be heading south in a day or so, and I don't think I'll be coming back.

"I've had it, chum."

14 Goodbye Ohoto

Neither Wilkinson nor I slept much the night following the nurse's confession. We walked for hours through a settlement shimmering under the luminescence of a full moon and echoing to the quaver of sled dogs tethered on the outskirts. Doug might have walked all night had we not seen a light in the Catholic rectory.

Father Choque opened the door to our tentative tap, brought out his last bottle of home-made raisin wine, and insisted we drink up.

"*Eh bien*. These are hard times, my friends," he said when he sent us on our way at last, "but surely good must come of it."

"I hope to hell he's right!" Doug muttered bleakly as we walked away. "I suspect the whole bloody mess will just get buried and conveniently forgotten."

The floodgates of his earlier reticence now opened wide and he unburdened himself about the multiple disasters that had afflicted "his people."

Although much of what he had to tell me concerned the Back River disaster, he was also anxious to help me delve into the Kikik tragedy. "I sat through her whole trial," he explained, "and we never really heard from Kikik herself. We saw it all from the outside looking in. You should go back to Eskimo Point and talk to her. I know she wasn't there when you went through before, but I hear she's there now."

Doug had also heard that all the surviving Ihalmiut were soon to be transported to Term Point, a remote and difficult-to-access peninsula on the Hudson Bay coast between Eskimo Point and Rankin Inlet.

"They'll be really isolated there. For their own good, of course. The likes of you, Farley, won't have a hope of getting close to them."

Doug then offered to fly me as far as Rankin.

"I haven't time to take you all the way and, anyway, there's no landing strip at Eskimo. But Easton will likely find a seat for you on some float plane heading south.

"We could leave tomorrow morning. The forecast is good though there's a radio blackout. No ionosphere layer to bounce signals back to earth. Big silent hole in the sky up there! Once airborne, we'll be out of the world for a few hours. Kind of a happy thought, eh?"

We left Baker very early next morning after loading two five-gallon jerry cans of gas into the Cub's tiny luggage compartment—just in case.

Everything else, including me and my gear, had to be squeezed into the narrow space behind the pilot. There being no room for sleeping bags, we left these basic pieces of survival gear behind on the runway.

It was a superb day for flying: calm and bright with only a few high-flung clouds between us and outer space. Because it is unwise to traverse large bodies of water in single-engined airplanes, we flew around the western end of Baker Lake.

We skimmed over Kanayook's fish camp where Charles Choque and I had spent a few days. No one came out of the tents to wave and I worried that the epidemic might have laid them all low. If so, there was nothing we could do about it. The kind of flying we were engaged in afforded a wonderful view of a world one could not touch.

Turning eastward along the lake's southern shore, we passed the mouth of the Kazan and overflew a single conical skin tent around which twenty or thirty caribou hides had been staked out to dry. This indication of a successful hunt cheered Doug so much he waggled the Cub's wings in an exuberant salute. At least we knew that some of the age-old People of the Deer were maintaining a semblance of their own way of life ... unless, of course, this was a ghost camp.

In due course the Cub touched down at Rankin—coincidentally with a bank of fog sweeping in off Hudson Bay. There was just time for me to hop out before Doug gunned the engine and was airborne again, heading home before the fog socked in solid. I walked into the settlement, hunted up Andy Easton, and explained my problem.

"Yeah, sure. You oughta go back to Eskimo Point. Get the lowdown before the bullshit blots it out. There's no float planes due here for a week." He thought for a moment. "But there's one guy could maybe get you there if you're fool enough to fly with him. Thousands wouldn't. But"—with a smile—"you might be dumb enough to chance it."

He introduced me to Keith, a would-be fighter ace lurking inside a mine accountant's body. Keith owned a Taylorcraft, a side-by-side two-seater of pre-war vintage with fabric-covered wings and fuselage. Although the plane looked as weary as a hen that has laid its last egg, Keith flew it as if it were a Spitfire.

Delighted with an excuse to get out of his office and into the high sky, he suggested we leave at once.

"But how are we going to land at Eskimo? I hear there's no strip there and your plane's on wheels."

"Not to worry, old son. There *was* an emergency strip there a few years back. If the Eskies haven't carried it off, we'll find it. Not to worry."

"Not to worry" was Keith's mantra.

We bounced out to the strip in a broken-down old truck and gassed up the Taylorcraft. Then Keith discovered the crankcase was almost empty. Not to worry. He rummaged in the back of the truck and came up with several cans of something called Rislone—an additive designed to loosen and flush away carbon deposits in gasoline engines.

"Not quite what the doctor ordered," he acknowledged with a grin. "But not to worry. It'll do."

We had been observed by the engineer of Easton's, Anson, who walked over to us.

"You know, fellas," he said as Keith emptied can after can of Rislone into the crankcase, "that might not be such a good idea. The engine in your little piss pot don't have no oil filter, and that stuff's goin' to stir up all the gunk and guck's been in her since she was built. I wouldn't do it, if I was you."

"Not to worry," Keith said over his shoulder, but the engineer was not to be so easily reassured.

"You listen sharp when you take off. Chances is you're goin' to hear squeak-squeak-squeak. Then it'll be SQUAWK-SQUAWK-SQUAWK. Then nothin' but the sound of the wind whistlin' through a seized-up prop. I wouldn't do it if I was you boys."

Keith was becoming irritated.

"I'll fly a couple of circuits well within gliding range of the strip, just to be sure."

Shaking his head, the engineer shambled away as we fired up the engine and took off. Simultaneously, a snowy owl perched on a hummock at the end of the strip launched itself into hurried flight, in the opposite direction.

When, after a few minutes, the engine showed no signs of stress, Keith abandoned the circuits and set course for Eskimo Point, 150 miles away to the south. There were some stutters from the engine, but no squeaks or squawks.

"Like I told you," Keith bellowed in my ear, "not to worry!"

Enormous flocks of snow geese gave the coastal flats the appearance of being already in winter's grip. The sleek white birds were drifting about in low flight against a tundra background suffused by early frost with a wash of molten copper, bronze, and gold.

Just before noon we raised the glitter of metal cladding on the roof of the Catholic church at Eskimo Point. Keith descended steeply towards the settlement. Soon we were almost at deck level, but I could see no sign of any airstrip. My anxiety must have been evident for Keith yelled:

"Not to worry, Farley. It'll be there when we need it. ... Hey, look! That must be it! That flat bit just behind the mission! Here we go!"

Alas, the flat bit was only part of a raised beach running through the settlement. Just before touching down, we became horrifyingly aware of a tent blocking the "runway." Keith gunned the engine and swung one wingtip up to clear the top of the tent while dipping the other into a ditch on the ocean side. Somehow the little plane clawed its way back upstairs.

Even Keith seemed somewhat taken aback, though not for long. He began to grin.

"Eskimo shamen used to go in big for tent-shaking. I think we might just have won top prize in that category!"

Now he banked inland to give the inhabitants of Eskimo Point time to collect themselves, and himself time to decide what to do next. Later, he told me his thoughts.

"If that *was* the old strip, it was no use to us. But we had to find something. We didn't have gas enough to get back to Rankin, or on to Churchill. I thought of ditching in the harbour, but I don't swim. Then I saw what looked like it *might* be an old airstrip. I couldn't be sure 'cause it was ass-deep in geese."

What Keith had spotted was a section of sandy esker that at some time had been roughly levelled for a few hundred yards. A man of instant decision, he dived towards it while flocks of indignant geese skittered out of the way on all sides.

Our wheels touched ... and sank into soft sand. The plane was about to pitch over on its nose when a gust of wind took it broadside and blew it off the top of the esker. Somehow my intrepid pilot regained flying speed and took us up again. Then he kicked the plane into a tight turn and headed down once more.

This time the Taylorcraft settled as prettily as a bird. The disturbed geese applauded by swooping back to land all around us. By the time we had scrambled out of the cockpit, we *were* almost ass-deep in them.

We were also separated from the settlement by two or three miles of bogs, ponds, and muskeg. However, now that I had safely returned to earth, the sound of icy mud and water sloshing about in my boots was sweet music to my ears.

I had reached my destination. But, as it turned out, not soon enough.

As Keith and I squelched our way into the community we encountered an acquaintance of mine, Sam Voisey, a seventy-eight-year-old trapper and one-time free trader. Sam told me that the Ihalmiut were being taken to Term Point that very *day* and that Kikik and some others had already been sent there. The remainder were to be loaded aboard a Peterhead boat. Meanwhile, they were still in the line of tents where I had found them on my prior visit.

"Like cattle waitin' to be sent to market," was how Sam angrily described them.

Sam Voisey was a long-timer in the Hudson Bay country, having come there in 1915 from his birthplace in Labrador. He had married a local Inuk woman and fathered several children, one of them being Henry Voisey, manager of Padlei Post. I had first met Sam in 1947 when I canoed into Eskimo Point. He seemed pleased to see me again.

"T'ain't the same place, me son. No more good times. Wait'll you meet King Billy! That's what we calls Bill Gallagher, the Mountie corporal. He's the boss around here, and you don't want to step on his toes or git in his way or you'll be some sorry!"

"Is he in charge of moving the Ennadai people?"

"That's right, bye. In charge o' every damn thing hereabouts."

"Then I'd better find him and state my case."

Sam grinned wolfishly. "Yiss, bye, and if you're still on your feet after, come around to the house and have a scoff."

Keith and I found the corporal on the beach. The policeman knew Keith and was polite to him, although he could not forbear from issuing a warning about low flying "over a populated area."

I was a different matter. He had heard about *People of the Deer*, and I was not on his list of admired authors. Barely acknowledging Keith's introduction, he demanded to know why I had come to Eskimo Point. And how soon I would be leaving.

"There's a TransAir Canso due here in an hour," he snapped. "I suggest you get on it. There may not be another chance to get out 'til winter. *If* you stay around you'll be strictly on your own. You can expect no favours from me."

I assured him I did not intend to remain in his bailiwick any longer than I had to.

"I've come to talk to the Ihalmiut woman, Kikik. I hear she's already gone out to Term Point so I'd like to board the Peterhead and go out there too. Then I'll guarantee to find my own way out of the country."

"I can't let you do that. Major Grant—he's the NSO for Term Point—is in my office. You *could* ask him, but you'd be wasting your time."

With which he strode imperiously away.

Keith grinned at the policeman's retreating back.

"Charming chap, ain't he? Well, I'd better get some gas and head for Rankin. If I was you, I'd catch a ride on the Canso. Being marooned in Eskimo Point with King Billy on your back ain't likely to be a barrel of fun. So long, pal, and not to worry."

Somewhat apprehensively I entered the detachment office. Major Grant turned out to be a bombastic type who had been out of the army about as long as I had, but was having trouble relinquishing the military image.

I introduced myself and made my request, only to have it ignored as the major launched into a panegyric about Term Point and what he proposed to do there.

"Ah, yes, Mr. Mowat. Want to know about Term Point? Well, it's a revolutionary project. It'll change the way things are done all over the Arctic. Solve a lot of problems for the natives. Let me tell you about it. ...."

He began by extolling the virtues of a Korean-style sewage system he planned to install in the model community he was going to build. Then he described his first industrial project—a factory to produce stoves capable of burning whale oil or peat or a combination of both. He may not have been aware that there were no sources of burnable peat in the region. Next he waxed lyrical about the greenhouses he intended to construct (presumably to be heated with whale oil and peat) as an object lesson for the Inuit in "agricultural diversification." He was especially enthusiastic about his plans to introduce modern technology, including machines of many kinds, "to take the misery out of the natives' lives."

When I interrupted in an attempt to get an answer to my request, he held up his hand imperiously and carried on.

"There will be remunerative work for everybody. The natural resources up here are absolutely unbelievable! We'll have native tradesmen skilled at cooking and canning exotic Arctic foods; trophy hunting of seals, walrus, polar bears, and whales by wealthy sportsmen! Won't get into the caribou just yet. They're scarce right now, though not"—and here he paused to chuckle appreciatively—"as scarce as Caribou Eskimos."

Attempting to humour him I nodded, but could not resist asking:

"Might there not be a bit of difficulty getting the inland Eskimos to adapt to such a changed way of life?"

It was the wrong question. He became every inch The Major.

"Not a bit of it! They can be taught! They *will* be taught! There'll be no more dole! Corporal Gallagher and I agree absolutely on that! They'll learn to earn their own keep! It's the only way they'll recover their self-respect!"

Unwisely, I risked another challenge. "Are you sure Term Point's the right site? Sam Voisey's trapped there for years. He's told me it's a very tough place to live. He says the harbour is hardly fit for even small boats."

"Utter nonsense! I've got a ten-thousand-ton freighter coming in there in a week's time! Got all our stuff aboard: trucks, dozers, Penguins [amphibious vehicles], prefab buildings, the lot."

I was distracted by the thunder of a Canso's twin engines overhead. It was decision-making time. I tried to regain lost ground.

"It all sounds very promising, Major. So, can I go along on the Peterhead and see for myself?"

"I don't believe so, Mr. Mowat. Not quite the right time, eh? Come back in a year or two, then we'll see."

Time was running out. The Canso had landed but was keeping its engines running. Sam Voisey had mail to go so I jumped aboard his canoe and rode out with him to the plane. The pilot, an ex-RAF type wearing a dirty white scarf around his neck, was sympathetic.

"Having a spot of trouble with the King, are we?" He grinned broadly. "Well, you just stay put, chum. I'll drop by on my way back from Chesterfield. Pick you up then and take you on to Churchill. Pip pip!"

Sam and I returned ashore, where he offered to accompany me to the Ihalmiut tents and act as interpreter.

"Gallagher'll blow a gasket if he sees us there. Hope he does! Let's go up to my cabin and have that scoff first."

The cabin, built mostly of salvaged lumber, was small, neat, and cozy. It had about it the welcoming atmosphere of a Newfoundland outport home. Sam's daughter, Rosie, acting as housekeeper, served us tea, fresh bread, and boiled trout, while his old and crippled wife smiled mistily at us from the corner.

"Gallagher hates my guts," said Sam with relish. "Like to drive me out of here, he would. He's tried, but I won't be drove."

"What's he got against you, Sam?"

"I don't hold with the way he treats the natives. He don't even allow drum-dances—which is about the only pleasure the poor folks has left.

Him and the priest is dead set against it. Calls it heathen practice! A while ago some of the inland people tried to have a little dance and he come along and took the drum from an old fellow was playing it, and smashed it on his knee. Then he picked the old feller up and shook him till he grunted. They'd been warned to stop, he told them; now they'd see he meant it."

I asked what he thought about the move to Term Point.

"This spring a fella from Ottawa flew in and asked some of us about that. I told him 'twas about the worst place on the coast to put them inland people. No deer out there at all. She's just a bald old chunk of rock poking twenty miles out to sea and twenty-five miles to the nearest fishing river.

"I've a winter tilt out there 'cause the point's good for white fox. Hardly nothin' else there in winter. The Ottawa fella, he says thank you very much and flies away. Next thing Bill Gallagher is telling us he's moving the inland people out to Term Point. Maybe if I'd told that Ottawa fella Term Point was Heaven on this earth, they woulda picked someplace else."

Sam and I made our way to the Ihalmiut tents as unobtrusively as possible. I admit to keeping an eye cocked for the redoubtable corporal, but he failed to materialize.

The fact that I was not accompanied by a representative of officialdom (it will be remembered that Special Constable Gibbons had been with me on my earlier visit) may have had something to do with the difference in my reception this time.

Yaha was positively garrulous, anxious to tell stories of life lived on the Barren Lands in happier times.

Hekwaw appeared to have recovered his wits and was full of anecdotes about old days and old ways. He spoke of musk ox hunts, of encounters near timberline with the *Itkilik* (Indians), and of month-long summer get-togethers of hundreds of Inuit on the shores of *Angikunituak*, the Great Lake on the Kazan.

"We sang and danced. We ate *Tuktu* until we could hardly belch. The children played all day and all night. We told stories. We made love. We fished. We picked berries. Sometimes we dreamed ... I remember ... I remember ..."

Sam and I were offered tea in all six tents. The people had precious little else to offer; nevertheless their condition seemed better than it had been during my earlier visit. Certainly they were in a better frame of mind.

"The hell of it is," Sam muttered in my ear, "they've got hold of the idea they're goin' back to Ennadai. They knows they're goin' someplace, and they wants to believe they're goin' home."

"Has nobody told them they're moving to Term Point ... *today?*" I asked incredulously.

"Not to my knowing. They'll be told that when it's time to march them down to the boat."

Ohoto, who had been off looking for berries, now arrived back at his tent. He greeted me enthusiastically, shaking hands *kablunak* fashion. Nanuk boiled the kettle and over more tea Ohoto talked about Kikik, who was his sister, describing what had happened to her.

I asked him how his sight was. No better, he told me. In fact, his blind eye was affecting the vision of the other one.

"He ought to go back to hospital," I said in an aside to Sam. "Without proper treatment he'll likely lose his good eye too."

"Yes, me son, they oughta send him out, but I doubt they will. It's Term Point for him and all his gang."

Ohoto picked up on the name and turned sharply to me.

"We go Term Point, Skibbee?"

I could have lied, but it was too late for that. When I failed to answer, Ohoto slowly turned away, nodded, and said softly, almost to himself:

"We not boss ... *ayoranamut*—nothing to be done."

A distant hum warned us that the Canso was coming. Sam and I stepped out of the tent and Ohoto followed. He put a hand on my shoulder and gave me his old familiar smile, one that had once seemed wide enough to engulf the whole world's sorrows.

There is no word for farewell in Inuktitut. Instead, he took his little soapstone pipe from his pocket and slipped it into mine.

"You go there, Skibbee," he said, pointing south. "We go there," pointing north towards Term Point. "... But I am dead inside."

The Canso touched down and Sam ferried me out to it. A few minutes later the plane was airborne. Peering out a salt-smeared window, I could dimly make out the Ihalmiut tents below. A squat figure was standing near them. Although he could not have seen me, I waved anyway.

Goodbye, Ohoto.

Epilogue

By the end of April 1958 officialdom had become uncomfortably aware of the magnitude of the disaster suffered by the inland people of Keewatin. Embarrassed politically, Ottawa moved in haste bordering on panic to implement a new policy. But what it came up with was only a variation on a ploy that had already failed the Ihalmiut three times. Another, but bigger and better, relocation decked out with bells and whistles was to be the answer to the problem of the dislocated and dispossessed People of the Deer.

The Department of Northern Affairs announced it would concentrate the remaining Ihalmiut together with the Haningaiormiut in a model "rehabilitation centre" to be located somewhere on the Hudson Bay coast between Churchill and Chesterfield. Here the famine survivors would be well housed; supplied with all essential needs in the way of food, clothing, medical attention, and education facilities; and, under the guidance of technical officers and NSOs, helped to achieve self-sufficiency as a prelude to joining the modern world.

Since time was of the essence, little was wasted in site selection. Nonala, Eskimo Point, Tavani, and Ferguson River—all of which offered easy access to the interior and to the caribou grounds—were considered, but the choice fell on Term Point. This was primarily because advisors from the Department of Public Works believed it would provide the most suitable building site and be readily accessible to large transport vessels.

On August 29 Major D. W. Grant shepherded his "happy little band" (as he called the Ihalmiut in one of his reports) ashore on Term Point's bleak headland. Two weeks later the MV *Maple Hill* arrived from Montreal, her holds crammed with cargo from which the new settlement was to be constructed.

Unable to enter the shallow, reef-strewn little harbour known as Whale Cove, the ship's master was forced to anchor off. When an autumnal storm blew up that night, *Maple Hill* had to put out to sea to avoid being blown ashore.

Returning on September 22, she again anchored off while her crew made a valiant attempt to ferry cargo ashore in motorized landing craft and barges. This proved an impossible task. Tides, currents, wind, and waves tossed the small vessels about, holing one landing craft, driving another ashore, and disabling the barges. Fewer than fifty tons of freight (mostly insulation in sodden and useless condition) was landed before another gale sprang up, again forcing *Maple Hill* back out to sea.

She never returned to Term Point. Instead, she steamed south to Churchill, there to land the bulk of her freight at the grain elevator wharf. And there it sat: of no more use to the involuntary settlers at Whale Cove than if it had remained in Montreal.

Early in October the Term Point site was abandoned. Sixteen Ihalmiut ended up spending the winter in a "traditional" tent camp on Wilson River, some thirty miles west of Whale Cove. The remainder were taken by Peterhead boat to the settlement at Rankin Inlet, on the outskirts of which DNA was now frantically trying to revive the Keewatin Re-establishment Project.

KRP, as it became known, consisted of a clutch of ten-by-twenty-foot plywood boxes (one for each Inuit family); a Quonset hut; two plywood "halls"; and, not least, a well-insulated, comfortably furnished, three-bedroom bungalow fitted with all modern conveniences to house the resident technical officer.

That winter KRP became home to thirty-seven Ihalmiut, about the same number of Haningaiormiut brought in from Baker Lake, and a few other destitute Inuit families.

According to a Rankin mine employee who was married to an Inuk and sympathetic to the plight of the Inuit:

"It was a refugee camp, pure and simple. Not the hell of a lot different from the DP [displaced persons] camps in Europe during the war. Like the DPs, the Eskimos at KRP had nothing, nowhere to go and nothing to do. They lived on government handouts. They were looked down on by just about everybody at Rankin, including Eskimos working in the mine. They were just about the most hopeless-looking lot I ever saw."

They were not, however, completely down and out.

Unable to endure KRP, they began drifting silently away, seeking a place where they would be spared the opprobrium of their own kind and could perhaps escape the arcane manipulations of the *kablunait*.

Neither the Ihalmiut nor the Haningaiormiut could go home—that possibility was closed to them forever. Perhaps because they could think of nowhere else to go, many Ihalmiut returned to Whale Cove where they seem to have found some comfort in the compassionate presence of old Sam Voisey and his family. Eventually they followed Sam back to Eskimo Point.

And that is where most of them ended their long journey.

One afternoon during her visit to Cape Breton, Kikik's daughter Elisapee Karetak and I examined a portfolio of photographs of her people that I had taken almost half a century earlier. As each face stared up at us from grainy black-and-white prints, Elisapee brought his or her story to its conclusion.

One of the first photos we looked at was of her mother. It showed Kikik, a tiny and remote figure, standing between two large *kablunait* during her trial at Rankin Inlet in 1958. Her face was expressionless: a blank mask revealing nothing of what she felt or had endured.

"She never ever talked about what happened," Elisapee told me, "not even to us children. She wanted everyone to forget. She didn't even want to associate with people who knew about it. A little while after the trial she married a Padliermio called Noah Kaikai, who lost his wife and all his children in the same starvation in 1958.

"They'd just got married when Kikik and us kids were X-rayed and all of us had TB and were sent south. We were sent to two different hospitals and put in different wards. My mother was gone two or three years and I hardly ever saw her. I was gone four years. I learned English and nearly forgot Inuktitut, and my name got changed to Elisapee.

"When she got back, Kikik and Noah had a baby. It was a son, but it died when it was only two. My mother died in 1972 of cervical cancer. She was in her early fifties, though nobody ever knew her real birthday."

What of the children Kikik had borne at Ennadai?

"My oldest sister, Ailouak, died in the winter of 1980. She was the one brought the knife when my mother was fighting Ootek. She remembered a lot, but wouldn't talk about it either. One day she just went out and never came back. The police called her death hypothermia, but she did not want to live any longer.

"My brother Karlak remembered some things, but did not want to, and did not want anyone to ever talk about what had happened. He got married and has four children. This last year he's changed, and now he agrees we have to bring everything out into the open and look at it together.

"My other sister, Annacatha, and I both got married too. Now the three of us and our kids all live in Arviat. It's our home, but now we've found our other home—Ennadai—we will never let it be forgotten."

As we leafed through the photos I learned that Ootek's wife, Howmik, had married again and borne three sons, but her crippled daughter, Kalak, who had been rescued from the starvation *iglu* at Henik Lake, had died in an institution in Winnipeg. Another daughter, Kooyak, grew up to marry a U.S. serviceman stationed at Churchill and is believed to live in Seattle—but she is lost to the people of Arviat.

Elisapee remembered that Yaha died "long ago," probably about 1962, "because he did not want to live any longer."

Miki—intractable son of an Ihalmio woman and a *kablunak*—lived until 1970. His son, David, is now a famous drummer in the traditional Inuit style and a moving spirit in attempts to revive something of the Ihalmiut heritage.

Owliktuk, that paragon of strength, survived until 1990 and his wife, Nutaralik, until 1998. Their son, Mounik, and his wife, Ookanak, are now the only remaining "elders" from the time when the Ihalmiut lived their own lives in their own land.

The last picture Elisapee and I came upon was a portrait of Ohoto, crouched in a canoe, holding a big lake trout. He was waving his knife in a mock-threat at me, the photographer, and grinning from ear to ear.

"He'd just caught that trout with my fishing rod," I explained to Elisapee, "and was daring me to try and claim it. That was Ohoto. Always a joker."

It was some time before Elisapee responded, and when she did her eyes were wet.

"He was my uncle, you know, and sometimes the only one I felt close to in Arviat. I loved him very much. When I felt real lonely, as if I didn't belong there because I had been away south for so long, he would be kind to me and make little jokes with me. ... So I loved him, but I guess not enough, because one winter he went away. ...

"He was completely blind by then. He and Nanuk had separated because he didn't want to be a trouble to anyone and he felt he wasn't able to look after things. Whenever I had the time I took him wherever he wanted to go—but he didn't want to depend on anybody. Sometimes he used to sit and talk to me. I was too young to remember what he talked about, but he was funny and he made me laugh when I felt like crying.

"Then one winter night in 1967 he went out of the community, got lost and froze to death ...

"That is what the police say happened."

"My Uncle did *not* get lost!
"He went walking on the land."

"Nobody had ever told me that when people believed they were of no more use, they could do that. So, you see, I didn't know.
"Now I understand."

INDEX